PORTRAIT OF THE BURNS COUNTRY
(and Galloway)

ALSO BY HUGH DOUGLAS

THE UNDERGROUND STORY
CROSSING THE FORTH
EDINBURGH
BURKE AND HARE

Portrait of
THE BURNS COUNTRY
(and Galloway)

HUGH DOUGLAS

PICTURES BY IAIN COATES

ROBERT HALE · LONDON

ISBN 0 7091 37850

Robert Hale & Company
63 Old Brompton Road
London S.W.7.

PRINTED IN GREAT BRITAIN BY
REDWOOD PRESS LIMITED
TROWBRIDGE, WILTSHIRE

CONTENTS

	Prefaces	**9**
I	Kyle for a Man	15
II	The Lie of the Land	39
III	Galloway—Cradle of Scotland	55
IV	Bonnie Fechters	70
V	Saints and Sinners	81
VI	Heroes of Scotland	99
VII	These Are The People	108
VIII	On Ayrshire Soil . . .	118
IX	A Separate and Avoided Tribe	128
X	Even African Chiefs Dance	142
XI	Marks of Man	150
XII	Immortal Memory	172
	Index	183

ILLUSTRATIONS

facing page

Alloway—the Auld Brig' O' Doon   16
Alloway—the cottage where Burns was born   17
Burns's father lies in Alloway Auld Kirkyard   17
Ayr—the Auld Brig' is still a busy thoroughfare   32
Burns means business in South-west Scotland   33
Ayr—Tam O' Shanter Inn, now a museum   48
Prestwick International Airport booking hall   49
Trees enhance Kyle's beauty   49
The road to Willie's Mill, Tarbolton   64
Lochlie, Burns's home for four years   64
The river Nith at Ellisland   65
Farm cat at Ellisland   80
Clatteringshaws Dam, part of Galloway power scheme   80
Caravans line the disused railway at Maidens   81
Sermon on the rocks below Girvan   81
Loch Trool, cradle of Scotland's nationhood   96
Bruce's Stone, Loch Trool
Poosie Nansie's Inn, Mauchline   *between pages*
Ploughing hillsides for new forests in   96 *and* 97
     Galloway

facing page

Mining, old style, at Waterside   97
Mining, new style, at Ochiltree   97
Scotland ends at the Mull of Galloway   112
Ailsa Craig dominates the Firth of Clyde   113

facing page

Portpatrick—now a quiet holiday resort	113
Machars landscape is wild and wind-swept	128
"The toil-worn Cotter frae his labour goes"	129
Dundrennan Abbey—sad beauty enfolded in the hills	144
Crossraguel Abbey—archways defy time	144
Football and bowls at Dalmellington	145
"Walking the dogs" at Dalbeattie	145
Miss Ellen McGavin knits Sanquhar pattern	160
Mr. Thomas Lochhead works at his potter's wheel in Kirkcudbright	160
Kirkcudbright—solid walls and cobbled streets	161
Dumfries—life revolves round the Midsteeple	176
"Here pause—and thro' the starting tear survey this grave . . ."—Burns's Mausoleum, Dumfries	177

PREFACE

A portrait means different things to different people; it can be a photographic likeness—warts and all—or it can be surrealist and attempt to express the personality behind the physical features of the sitter. This portrait attempts something between the two—to give a picture of the appearance of my native country as it is today, and to show the history that has made the people and the place what they are.

Burns may have made the South-west, but the South-west also made Burns. He was influenced by Wallace and Bruce, whose country this is also, and by the Lollards and Covenanters who lived there in centuries before him. And this is not a land of one poet, but of a thousand verse-makers before and after the time of Burns.

I was overjoyed to be invited to write this portrait of my native countryside. Yet the task filled me with awe, for how can one impart that deep love for one's homeland that goes far beyond mere words? If I have succeeded it is thanks to the many willing helpers I have had. The Librarians and their staff at the county libraries of Ayr, Dumfries, Kirkcudbright and Wigtown have all helped, and I am especially indebted to Mr James Forsyth, Librarian of Ayr Carnegie Library who spared no trouble to locate books and supply information. The County Clerks and their staffs, the staff of local firms, and the people of the South-west in general have helped me with characteristic kindness, and I thank them.

Of course the many histories of the South-western counties have been invaluable, and I owe a special debt to Charles Dougall, who carried out a similar labour of love sixty years ago. I have quoted from the *Guide to Glen Trool Forest Park* by kind permission of its publishers, Her Majesty's Stationery Office, and Mr John R. Allan has given me permission to quote from his book *Summer in Scotland*.

I would like to express my special thanks to my mother who drove me around the Burns Country and Galloway and waited patiently while I gathered my material. Iain Coates took the pictures. My wife, John Stocks and Jean Land read the proofs, and my family and friends encouraged me throughout the task. This book is as much theirs as mine. Together

> We'll sing auld Coila's plains an' fells,
> Her moors red-brown wi' heather bells,
> Her banks an' braes, her dens an' dells,
>   Whare glorious Wallace
> Aft bure the gree, as story tells,
>   Frae Suthron billies.

HUGH DOUGLAS
February 1968

PREFACE TO THE SECOND EDITION

In four years much has changed in the Burns Country, and yet the more one looks at these changes the more one realises that the character of my homeland remains the same. In revising the book I have once again met with unfailing kindness and helpfulness on all sides.

H.D.
April 1972

To
all those Ayrshire folk
who are my kith and kin
and especially to
ALLAN and MARION RAMSAY
who know and love
the Burns Country and Galloway

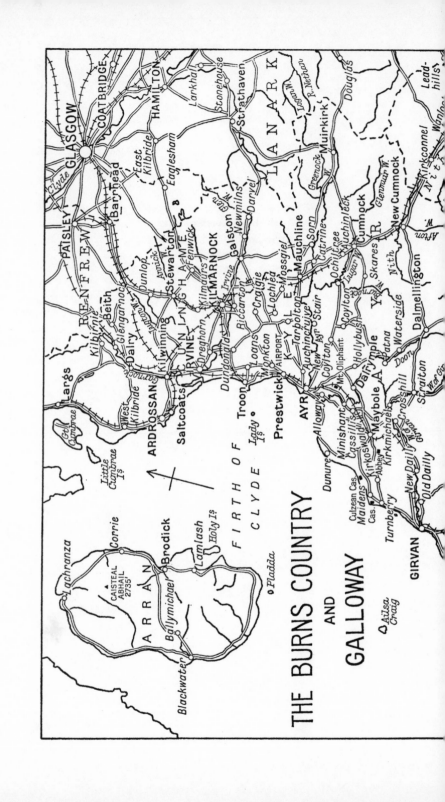

THE BURNS COUNTRY

AND

GALLOWAY

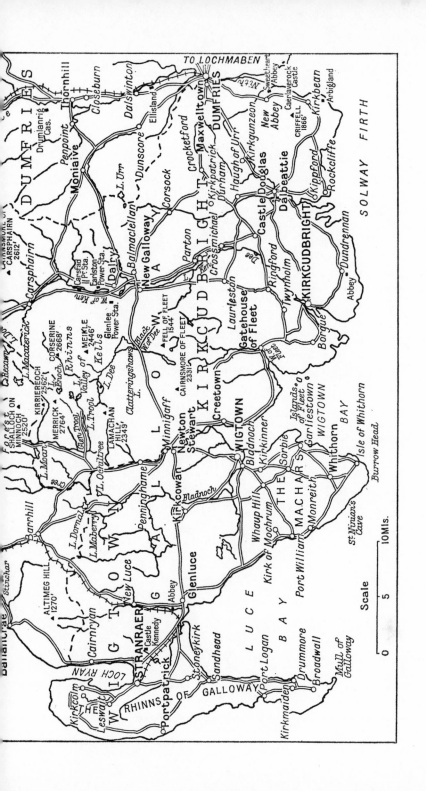

KYLE FOR A MAN

SUMMER days linger in Scotland as if loath to leave, and that half hour between day and night is a time of serenity and great beauty. Nowhere is the gloaming more beautiful than over the Firth of Clyde where one may stand on the Ayrshire coast, by the broad estuary, and watch the sun redden and set behind the Island of Arran. At that moment a hundred brilliant shades of red and orange colour the sky and Arran's peaks are silhouetted so clearly that it is easy to see how the Sleeping Warrior received its name. Turning left, and southwards, Ailsa Craig vanishes, and the sharp lines of the Heads of Ayr soften and merge into the night. Suddenly one becomes aware of the lighthouses of Pladda, Holy Isle and the Lady Isle peering back through the darkness, guiding ships up and down the Firth, for this water is not the end of a great river, but the beginning of a high road from Scotland to Ireland, England, and the whole world.

The lazy lapping of the sea on the sand is now drowned by the roar of aircraft, and, turning, one sees navigation lights winking back messages as the pilot sets his course across the Firth, over Arran and out of sight. Here is another and newer highway from Ayrshire, for the aeroplane is embarking on a journey from Prestwick International Airport, the crossroads of Scotland.

As the eye follows the plane's lights, the mind asks many questions. Is it bound for New York? Montreal? Or Boston, perhaps?

Does it carry emigrants who have seen their homeland vanish into the darkness, or tourists returning from a visit to Scotland? One cannot answer these questions for sure, nor, on the other hand, can one be contradicted on the answers one's mind offers.

However, one thing is certain—some of the departing tourists had been lured to Scotland by a legend which was founded not far from this point on the Ayrshire coast; they had come to visit the homeland of Robert Burns.

There is a rhyme about the South-west of Scotland, which sums up the ancient feudal baillieries which it once comprised. It goes:

> Kyle for a man;
> Carrick for a coo;
> Cunningham for butter and cheese;
> And Galloway for 'oo.

Ayr is in the heart of Kyle; the rolling, hillocky centre of the county. Cunningham lies to the north, most of it beyond the scope of this portrait, and Carrick is to the south, with Galloway stretching beyond, all the way to the Solway Firth. 'Kyle for a man', says the rhyme. 'Kyle for *a* man', echoes the world, for this is the land of Robert Burns, Scotland's ploughman poet and national bard.

Burns was born in Kyle, although neither his father nor his mother had their origins there. Agnes Broun was the daughter of a Carrick farmer, and William Burnes (for that was how the earlier generations of the family spelled the name), had been born at Clochnahill, Kincardineshire. Like so many Scottish farmers' sons of the time, William Burnes grew up to find there was no livelihood for him among his own folk, so he hied south to Edinburgh and then to Ayrshire where he became gardener to Mr. Crawford of Doonside and then to Dr. William Fergusson at Doonholm, both close to Alloway.

Here William met Agnes Broun, a happy, dark-eyed farmer's daughter from Maybole, and for her he built a cottage on a few

Alloway—the Auld Brig' O' Doon

acres of land which he had leased at Alloway. When the cottage was ready William and Agnes were married and settled down to turn it into a home. Thirteen months later, on the 25th January 1759, their first child was born in a tiny bed recessed off the kitchen in so small and dark a space that it is no more than a hole in the wall. They named their son Robert. Later Robert was to celebrate his own birth and to assess his impact on the community in verse. There was much truth in what he wrote:

> He'll hae misfortunes great and sma',
> But aye a heart aboon them a';
> He'll be a credit till us a',
> We'll a' be proud o' Robin.'

Today Scotland is more than proud of Robin—Alloway is a shrine and the cottage a literary altar before which the world kneels. The house has been restored to its original appearance, and pilgrims walk through the barn and byre into the room and kitchen—the but and the ben—which was the Burnes family's home until they outgrew it and moved to Mount Oliphant. In the cottage at Alloway you can see the original timbers, the ingle where Mrs. Burnes's sweet voice harmonised with the pots hanging on the 'swee', the dresser laden with crockery, the grandfather clock, and of course the box bed in which the poet was born. Basically the house did not differ greatly from many farmhouses in Ayrshire until the last century brought affluence to farmers and grander ideas to their wives. The kitchen of the farmhouse where I was born, some five miles from Alloway, also had a big open fireplace to which a Victorian range had been added, and cement covered the earthen floor which my mother remembers as a child. The dresser was stacked with crockery, and a grandfather clock 'chapped' the hours. Two box beds opened on to the kitchen and, although I was not born in either of them, my sister recalls that in her excitement to see her new brother she fell out of one of them and raised a large lump on her forehead which the maid smeared with butter. The box beds were removed in the name of progress—

2

Alloway—the cottage where Burns was born
Burns's father lies in Alloway Auld Kirkyard

as were the open range and cement floor in turn—but the dresser and grandfather clock remained until we left the house a few years ago.

At Alloway there has been gathered a superb collection of furniture, personal possessions and books connected with the poet. A museum at the back of the cottage houses most of these, although many items which have little direct connection with the poet clutter the cottage and spoil its authentic look of the time when William Burnes occupied it.

In the 1760s the Burnes family filled the cottage at Alloway to overflowing, too, and to provide for his growing family William took over the lease of Mount Oliphant, a farm only two miles away high above Ayr and with superb views across the town and the Firth of Clyde. The land of Kyle yields well enough today, but in the eighteenth century it was both sour and dour, and it claimed the lives of both William Burnes and Robert.

William Burnes had a Scotsman's respect for learning, and by the time Robert was six he was trotting off to school at Alloway Mill each day. When the schoolmaster left to take up another appointment it was William who went to Ayr and engaged John Murdoch to school his children and those of his neighbours. Five families accommodated the new master in turns, and they garnered enough money amongst them to pay his salary. John Murdoch was no more than a dozen years older than his solemn, dark-eyed pupil, and a tremendous bond grew between the two. Murdoch wrote of the poet and his brother:

"Robert and Gilbert were generally at the upper end of the class, even when ranged with boys by far their seniors. The books most commonly used in the school were the *Spelling Book*, the *New Testament*, *The Bible*, *Masson's Collection of Prose and Verse*, and *Fisher's English Grammar*." Murdoch's pupils worked diligently. "As soon as they were capable of it, I taught them to turn verse into its natural prose order; and sometimes to substitute synonymous expressions for poetical words, and to supply all the ellipses."

When it came to music, however, the pair were left far behind. "Robert's ear, in particular, was remarkably dull, and his voice untuneable," complained Murdoch. "It was long before I could get them to distinguish one tune from another."

Murdoch continued to teach his pupils for two years after they left Alloway for Mount Oliphant, but when he had to leave Alloway schooling stopped, apart from lessons from their father by candlelight on winter evenings, and a short spell one summer when Robert and Gilbert were sent week about to school at Dalrymple—week about because their father could not spare both of them from the farm, and he probably could not afford two sets of fees either. When Murdoch returned to Ayr Robert was released from farmwork for a few weeks so that he could revise his English grammar, and now he met boys who were able to lend him books which he himself could never have afforded. At this time he was also given a brief introduction to the French language, and had a rather less successful encounter with Latin.

Sketchy as it may sound today when children have eleven or more unbroken years of schooling, Robert had a good education for his time. He was not the unlettered ploughman which he afterwards let people in Edinburgh think him; Robert was well educated compared with other boys of similar background and, of course, his brilliant mind enabled him to make the most of every scrap of Murdoch's teaching.

His own genius and book learning were the natural elements. Yet some catalyst was needed to transmogrify them into the precious substance of poetry. Three catalysts were there.

First, his mother's constant singing must have made more impression on Burns than all Murdoch's tuition in church music. Next was an old woman who came about the house, Betty Davidson, whose tales frightened him and set his childish imagination to work. Betty's tales cultivated the latent seeds of poetry Burns wrote later, but they "had so strong an effect on my imagination that to this hour, in my nocturnal rambles, I sometimes keep a sharp look-out in suspicious places; and though nobody can be more sceptical than I am in such matters, yet it often takes an effort of philosophy to shake off these idle terrors."

The third catalyst was Nelly Kilpatrick, the first girl to turn his head to love and poetry. "You know our country custom of coupling a man and woman together as partners in the labours of harvest," wrote Burns later as he looked back to his connection with Nelly. "In my fifteenth autumn my partner was a bewitching creature who just counted an Autumn less. My scarcity of English denies me the power of doing her justice in that language, but you know the Scottish idiom—she was a bonnie, sweet sonsie lass. In short she, altogether unwittingly to herself, initiated me in a certain delicious passion which, in spite of acid disappointment, gin-horse prudence, and book-worm philosophy, I hold to be the first of human joys, our dearest blessing here below. . . . I did not know myself why I liked so much to loiter behind with her, when returning in the evening from our labours; why the tones of her voice made my heart-strings thrill like an Aeolian harp; and, particularly why my pulse beat such a furious ratan, when I looked and fingered over her little hand, to pick out the cruel nettle stings and thistles. . . . Thus with me began love and poesy. . . ."

Nell's sweet voice appealed to Robert; especially as she taunted him with a song which another of her swains had composed to her. For the first time Robert "committed the sin of verse", when he composed a song to fit Nell's favourite reel tune . . .

> O once I lov'd a bonie lass,
> Aye, and I love her still;
> And whilst that virtue warms my breast,
> I'll love my handsome Nell.

Those moments in the harvest field with Nell and the long hours spent reading or rhyming in the evening were little enough reward for the hardship of life at Mount Oliphant. Gilbert remembered these days thus: "For several years butcher's meat was a stranger in the house, while all the members of the family exerted themselves to the utmost of their strength and rather beyond it, in the labours of the farm. My brother, at the age of thirteen, assisted in thrashing the crop of corn, and at fifteen was the principal labourer on the farm, for we had no hired servant, male or female. The anguish of mind we felt at our tender years, under these straits and difficulties was very great. To think of our father growing old (for he was now above fifty), broken down with the long-continued fatigues of his life, with a wife and five other children, and in a declining state of circumstances, these reflections produced in my brother's mind and mine sensations of deepest distress."

At this time also came the first signs of the illness which was to dog Robert's footsteps. Said Gilbert: "He was almost constantly afflicted in the evenings with a dull headache, which, at a future period of his life, was exchanged for a palpitation of the heart, and a threatening of fainting and suffocation in his bed, in the night-time."

Breaks were few—the time spent with his old teacher in Ayr and a few weeks in Kirkoswald to learn "mensuration, surveying, and dialling." In Kirkoswald he learnt also about smuggling, and public house "scenes of swaggering riot and roaring dissipation" until "a charming fillette . . . overset my trigonometry, and set me off in a tangent from the sphere of my studies." This time the girl was Peggy Thomson, and how she captivated him! "It was vain to think of doing any more good at school. The remaining week I staid, I did nothing but craze the faculties of my soul about her, or steal out to meet her; and the last two nights of my stay in the country, had sleep been a mortal sin, the image of this modest and innocent girl had kept me guiltless." Again he turned to poesy:

—Peggy dear, the evening's clear,
Thick flies the skimming swallow;
The sky is blue, the fields in view,
All fading green and yellow:
Come, let us stray our gladsome way,
And view the charms of nature;
The rustling corn, the fruited thorn,
And every happy creature.

Life was always hard for William Burnes; now it became impossible. On the death of his old employer, Dr. Fergusson, who had lent him money to stock Mount Oliphant, Burnes was hounded and threatened by the factor responsible for collecting the money. When a break in the lease at last gave Burnes the chance to quit he moved to Lochlie, near Tarbolton, seven or eight miles inland. Here the soil was no better than that which he had left, but for a time at least the move gave him respite. Work was still hard and the day's toil long, and the move cut Robert off from his Ayr friends, so he turned out less poetry than he might have done. But soon he gathered together a new set of men who were to be important influences on his life both then and later. Among them were David Sillar, a poet of sorts; John Rankine, a fellow farmer; James Findlay, an exciseman who was later to introduce Robert to the work; Saunders Tait, a tailor with a temper and a taste for scandal, who later turned against Robert; and of course poor John Wilson, the schoolmaster, who had to eke out his living with a grocer's shop and by acting as apothecary to the townsfolk. It was this last pursuit that made him the butt of Burns's satire in the poem "Death and Dr. Hornbrook", which related the story of an encounter between the two just down the road from Willie's Mill at Tarbolton. Death bemoaned the fact that there was no chance for him to exercise his powers thereabouts since the doctor killed off everyone first.

Robert's life soon expanded, but not always to the pleasement of his father, who feared until his dying day, for his son's future. William Burnes took great exception to Robert's attending a country dancing class. About this same time the poet became a Freemason and took the initiative in forming the famous Tarbolton Bachelors' Club, a debating and literary society run by the poet and his friends. The Bachelors' Club had a long set of rules which show evidence of Robert's hand—especially the tenth one:

Every man proper for a member of this Society, must have a frank, honest, open heart; above any thing dirty or mean; and must be a professed lover of one or more of the female sex. No haughty, self-conceited person, who looks upon himself as superior to the rest of the Club, and especially no mean-spirited, worldly mortal, whose only will is to heap up money, shall upon any pretence whatever be admitted. In short, the proper person for this Society is, a cheerful, honest-hearted lad; who, if he has a friend that is true, and a mistress that is kind, and as much wealth as genteely to make both ends meet —is just as happy as this world can make him.

At each meeting a subject was debated, and here again Robert's hand is evident. The subject for 11th November 1780, is recorded in his handwriting:

Suppose a young man, bred a farmer, but without any fortune, has it in his power to marry either of two women, the one a girl of large fortune, but neither handsome in person, nor agreeable in conversation, but who can manage household affairs of a farm well enough; the other of them a girl every way agreeable in person, conversation, and behaviour, but without any fortune; which of them shall he choose?

Robert's line of argument in that debate is not hard to guess at. Of his attitude to women at this time he wrote, "*Vive l'amour et vive la bagatelle*, were my sole principles of action." His friend David Sillar confirms his great facility for conversing with girls they met on walks in the fields between kirk sermons on Sundays. "Many times when I have been bashfully anxious how to express myself," wrote Sillar, "he would have entered into conversation with them with the greatest ease and freedom; and it was generally a death blow to our conversation, however agreeable, to meet a female acquaintance."

Robert and his brother rented some land from their father to grow flax, and they were successful enough at this for Robert to win a prize of three pounds. Much of their profit was going to the middleman, the flax-dresser, however, so Robert decided to go to Irvine in the summer of 1781, and learn to dress his own flax. Like so many of Robert's plans the scheme went agley, misfortunes piled up until he was depressed and ill, and finally on New Year's morning, 1782, the workshop belonging to him and his partner was burned down. Robert lingered a while in Irvine and returned to Lochlie the following spring.

At Irvine Burns met a young sailor called Richard Brown. "He was the only man I ever saw who was a greater fool than myself, where woman was the presiding star," wrote Burns of his friend, "but he spoke of a certain fashionable failing with levity—which hitherto I had regarded with horror. Here his friendship did me a mischief."

Nonetheless, Brown encouraged him in his poetry and into thinking about publishing some of it. Burns was writing little at this time "but meeting with Fergusson's Scotch 'poems'," he reports, "I strung anew my wildly-sounding lyre with emulating vigor." Now flowed poems like "My Nanie O" and "Green Grow the Rashes O".

At Lochlie matters worsened. William Burnes, who never had a written lease for his tenancy of the farm, became involved in a long, complicated lawsuit over alleged arrears of rent and, although he won his case at the Court of Session in Edinburgh, it cost him all his money to "the hell-hounds who growl in the kennels of justice". He was now an old, broken and ruined man, and death could not wait long to claim him. He died on 13th February 1784, and was buried in the Auld Kirkyard at Alloway, close to the cottage where he had embarked on married life a quarter of a century before.

Lochlie had grown sour, and the Burns family were thankful to accept from Gavin Hamilton of Mauchline a sub-lease of Mossgiel, a farm a few miles away, nearer Mauchline. The family moved there a month after their father's death.

Robert was now head of the household and as such he was determined to succeed. "I entered this farm, with a full resolution," he wrote. "Come, go, I will be wise! I read farming books; I calculated crops; I attended markets . . . but the first year from unfortunately buying bad seed, and the second from a late harvest, we lost half our crops. This overset all my wisdom, and I returned like 'the dog to his vomit, and the sow that was washed to her wallowing in the mire'." The truth is Robert was not a farmer; his hand may have been firm enough at the plough, but his heart was singing all the while with Ramsay, Fergusson, and every other poet. Robert Burns was turning irrevocably towards poetry, and the years at Mossgiel saw the composition of much of his best work.

Burns's muse ranged widely—sometimes his theme was a bonnie lass, sometimes a comment on the people and world around him, but often it was scalding satire on iniquities of eighteenth-century Ayrshire, especially on the Kirk.

In the West of Scotland at that time a kind of civil war was splitting the Presbyterian Church. On the one hand sat the stern, unyielding Calvinists who held to the tenet of predestination— that is to say that a few are pre-ordained to salvation regardless of the lives they lead, while all others are destined to purgatory and are powerless to alter this destiny. These Auld Lichts, as they were called, were opposed by the New Lichts, the more liberal-minded kirkmen. Burns sided with the New Lichts, but the feud touched him both through his own erring and through the quarrel be- tween his landlord, Gavin Hamilton and the Auld Lichts in general and the Rev. Dr. William Auld—'Daddy' Auld, guardian of the Mauchline folks' souls—in particular. This feud resulted in two of Burns's greatest poems, "Holy Willie's Prayer" and "The Holy Fair", both satires on the Auld Lichts. "Holy Willie" was an elderly stalwart of 'Daddy' Auld's Kirk, and in the poem Burns was eavesdropping on him at his prayers. Willie addressed his Maker:

> O Thou that in the heavens does dwell,
> Wha, as it pleases best Thysel',
> Sends ane to heaven an' ten to hell,
>   A' for thy glory.
> And no for onie guid or ill
>   They've done before Thee.

Willie was confident that God had chosen him one of his elect, predestined to salvation:

> Yet I am here a chosen sample,
> To show thy grace is great and ample;
> I'm here a pillar o' thy temple,
>   Strong as a rock,
> A guide, a buckler, and example,
>   To a' thy flock.

Willie had sinned and he confessed it—he had lifted a 'lawless leg' over Meg, and he had lain with Leezie's lass (but of course he had drink taken or he would never have done so). His confession ended, Willie set about Hamilton.

> Lord, mind Gaw'n Hamilton's deserts;
> He drinks, an' swears, an' plays at cartes,
> Yet has sae mony takin arts,
>   Wi' great and sma'
> Frae God's ain priest the people's hearts
>   He steals awa'

> An' when we chasten'd him therefor,
> Thou kens how he bred sic a splore[1],
> And set the world in a roar
>   O' laughing at us;
> Curse Thou his basket and his store,
>   Kail and potatoes.

There is an Old Testament ring to the whole poem, but especially to the last smug verse as Willie ends his prayer:

> But Lord, remember me an' mine
> Wi' mercies temporal and divine,
> That I for grace an' gear may shine,
>   Excelled by nane[2],
> And a' the glory shall be Thine,
>   Amen, Amen.

[1] uproar.
[2] none.

"Holy Willie's Prayer" breached the walls of the fortress of Calvinism; "The Holy Fair" was the final assault. For his satire Burns chose to describe one of these Holy Fairs, or great outdoor Communion meetings, which were still held in the West of Scotland in the eighteenth-century. From all sides the faithful and the faithless, the elect and the damned, gathered to hear a torrent of Auld Licht preaching. Deftly the scene was summed-up as the poet passed the collection plate presided over by a glowering elder, to join the throng:

> Here stands a shed to fend the show'rs,
>   'An screen our countra gentry;
> There Racer Jess[1], an' two-three whores,
>   Are blinkin' at the entry;
> Here sits a raw o' tittlin' jads,
>   Wi' heavin breasts an' bare neck;
> An' there a batch o' wabster[2] lads,
>   Blackguardin frae Kilmarnock,
>   For fun this day.
>
> Here some ar thinkin on their sins,
>   An' some upo' their claes[3];
> Ane curses feet that fyl'd[4] his shins,
>   Anither sighs and prays:
> On this hand sits a chosen swatch[5]
>   Wi' screw'd-up, grace-proud faces;
> On that a set o' chaps, at watch,
>   Thrang[6] winkin on the lasses
>   To chairs that day.

[1] daughter of Manchline inn-keeper Poosie Nancy.
[2] weaver.
[3] clothes.
[4] dirtied.
[5] sample.
[6] busy.

And what do the 'grace-proud faces' gaze upon? The improvised pulpit from which a never-ending succession of preachers hurl an endless assault on sin. Listen to one:

> Hear how he clears the points o' Faith
>   Wi' rattlin and thumpin.
> Now meekly calm, now wild in wrath,
>   He's stampin, an' he's jumpin.
> His lengthen'd chin, his turn'd up snout,
>   His eldrich squeel and gestures,
> O how they fire the heart devout—
>   Like cantharidian plaisters
>   On sic a day.

When Smith begins his 'cauld harangues' on practice and morals the godly have had enough, and flock to the refreshment tent. Already things are hectic there:

> The lads and lassies, blythely bent
>   To mind baith saul an' body,
> Sit round the table, weel content,
>   An steer[1] about the toddy:
> On this one's dress, an' that anes leuk[2]
>   They're making observations,
> While some are cozie i' the neuk[3]
>   An' formin assignations
>   To meet some day.

But no matter how hard the ministers preach and how contrite every sinner may seem when the holy fair is over, the ending will be the same.

[1] stir.
[2] look.
[3] corner.

How mony hearts this day converts
  O' sinners and o' lasses
Their hearts o' stane, gin night,[1] are gane
  As soft as ony flesh is;
There's some are fou o' love divine;
  There's some are fou o' brandy;
An mony[2] jobs that day begin
  May end in houghmagandie[3]
                Some ither day.

These poems and others like "Address to the Deil", and the "Address to the Unco Guid", set 'Daddy' Auld and the elders in a frenzy. Burns himself described the kirk session's alarm as such "that they held several meetings to look over their spiritual artillery, and see if any of it might be pointed against profane rhymers", Indeed, Robert was a target they could scarcely miss; while his father lay dying Elizabeth Paton was brought in to help in the house at Mossgiel and, although a plain enough lass, she fell before Robert's amorous onslaught and in May 1785, bore his child. Burns had scarcely greeted his 'love-begotten daughter' than Jean Armour, one of the belles of Mauchline, also fell before him. This time it appears he intended to marry the girl he had wronged, and indeed he and Jean pledged their marriage and signed a document confirming it, which was enough in Scots law at that time to constitute a binding marriage. Indeed, such 'marriages by consent' without paper confirmation remained valid in Scotland up to 1939. Jean's father did not accept the situation as placidly as his daughter did, for he had the written evidence of the marriage destroyed and packed Jean off to relatives in Paisley. Despite all the precautions of the Armours, 'Holy Willie' Fisher and his 'houghmagandie pack' began to sniff the scent, and Robert made plans to escape by emigrating to Jamaica.

[1] by night.
[2] many.
[3] fornication.

Rejected by Jean and hounded by her father Robert fell for Mary
Campbell, a Highland servant girl at Gavin Hamilton's house.
The Highland Mary affair was as passionate as it was brief, and
mysterious. We know that on the second Sunday of May 1786,
the two met by the River Ayr and there are said to have exchanged
Bibles—at least Robert gave Mary a Bible which can now be seen
at Burns's Monument in Alloway. Mary then went home to her
parents in Campbeltown, but in the late Autumn she returned to
Greenock where she died—giving birth to Robert's child if tradition is true (and we are by no means certain that it is true). And by
this time Jean Armour had given birth to twin children whom he
acknowledged as his own.

In the midst of all this confusion Burns decided to publish his
poems to pay his passage to the West Indies, and this changed
every plan. Towards the end of July 1786, *Poems Chiefly in the
Scottish Dialect* appeared—a rare volume called the Kilmarnock
edition today because it was printed by John Wilson in Kilmarnock. The book was an immediate success. Robert Heron wrote:
"Old and young, high and low, grave and gay, learned and
ignorant, were alike delighted, agitated, transported. I was at that
time resident in Galloway, contiguous to Ayrshire, and I can well
remember how even ploughboys and maid-servants would have
gladly bestowed the wages they earned the most hardly, and which
they wanted to purchase necessary clothing if they might procure
the Works of Burns." And if the poor seized on the new
poet's work with enthusiasm, so too did the rich and famous,
Professor Dugald Stewart of Edinburgh, Mrs. Dunlop of Dunlop,
and Dr. Thomas Blacklock the blind poet, among them. Now he
went off to Edinburgh to arrange the publication of a new edition,
and here he was lionised by aristocrats and intellectuals. The
ploughman poet was the wonder of the capital, and Robert loved
this adulation and allowed the image to grow.

In the Edinburgh days, too, there was a succession of women.
The affairs were sometimes of the heart, sometimes of the head,
but occasionally a bit of both. Mrs. Dunlop of Dunlop, whose

friendship ended in estrangement because of Burns's republican and revolutionary sympathies, appealed to his intellect. Jenny Clow and Meg Cameron appealed to the flesh, and produced bastard children to prove it. Mrs. Agnes Maclehose came somewhere between heart and head, although there was a good amount of passion in their relationship. How else could their association have produced the beautiful:

> Had we never lov'd sae kindly!
> Had we never lov'd sae blindly!
> Never met—or never parted,
> We had ne'er been broken hearted.

After two seasons in Edinburgh broken by tours of the Borders, the Highlands and Stirlingshire, and brief visits home, he had another two volumes of poems in print. He had achieved even more—Jean Armour was again expecting his child, and was driven out of her father's house. At first Robert had no intention of acknowledging their earlier marriage, but suddenly, inexplicably, he turned about, married her, and this time obtained the kirk's blessing. Again Jean was delivered of twins, but they died within a day or two.

Why did Burns change his mind about marriage? It would be uncharitable to suggest that he had leased the farm of Ellisland, near Dumfries, and needed a housekeeper. On Jean's part it would be unkind to say that she needed a father for her bairns and a roof to cover her head. Possibly the truth is that both realised at last that their future lay together. Burns could hardly have chosen a more suitable wife. Although Jean was not able to share his intellectual interests she was a good wife, who understood his failings, accepted them, and made no effort to change him. Jean probably knew her husband's real worth, and accepted him as he was.

Robert loved her, too, and as he worked to build a house for her on his new farm he missed her badly. His longing to be with her was expressed in song:

> Of a' the airts[1] the wind can blaw,
>   I dearly like the west,
> For there the bonnie Lassie lives,
>   The Lass I lo'e the best:
> There's wild-woods grow, and rivers row,
>   And mony a hill between;
> But day and night my fancy's flight
>   Is ever wi' my Jean.

The year 1788 had nearly closed before the house was ready and he was able to bring his Jean home to Ellisland. The first days together were among the happiest of his whole life. He was overjoyed to have his wife beside him, and said so:

> I see thee dancing o'er the green,
> Thy waist sae jimp[2], thy limbs sae clean,
> Thy tempting lips, thy roguish een—
>   By Heaven and Earth I love thee!

Although Burns never lost the art of satire, another form of poesy now came to occupy him more and more. In Edinburgh he encountered James Johnson, who was then compiling the first volume of his *Scots Musical Museum*, and Burns seized on the project with delight. He contributed many songs to subsequent volumes, and song-making became an important part of his life. Later he was to help George Thomson to compile his collection of *Select Scottish Airs*, and of course the result was a heritage of song such as no other nation possesses. Burns "collected, begged, borrowed and stole" every song he could find; he refurbished old words, composed new words where necessary, and sometimes even wrote original words to a tune which hitherto had none.

Burns left us more than three hundred songs, so many of them deserving mention that it is hard to know where to begin even to list them—"Auld Lang Syne" has become an international song of

[1] directions.
[2] slender.

Ayr—the Auld Brig' is still a busy thoroughfare

BURNS EMPORIUM
EWSAGENT   TOBACCONIST

CAPSTAN MEDIUM CIGARETTES

Rabbie's

Restaurant   Bar

LAND O' BURNS BAKERIE

OVEN FRESH BREAD

LAND O' BURNS
PHONE AYR & PRESTWICK 79210
(THE ADVANCED)
MOTORING SCHOOL

parting; "Scots Wha Hae" is practically our national anthem (at least it is the expression of our nationhood); and from some Jacobite scraps he moulded "A Man's a Man For A' That", a sentiment which appeals greatly to the Scot. But it was at the love song that he excelled as he ranged from a young girl's love in "I'm Ower Young to Marry Yet", to the deep affection of old age in "John Anderson, My Jo". As in his real-life love-making, there was no airy romanticising in the love songs. He knew what he wanted to say and he said it—basically and beautifully. When he loved Annie Rankin in the harvest field he told the world:

> I ken't her heart was a' my ain,
>   I lov'd her most sincerely;
> I kissed her owre, and owre again,
>   Amang the rigs o' barley.

His love songs are numerous—as indeed are the people about whom they are supposed to have been written. One wonders how he could have loved all the girls he wrote about, or if he did, how he managed to find time to set pen to paper about them. Whatever the truth of the incidents that inspired them we are grateful for songs like "Mary Morison", "O Wert thou in the Cauld Blast", and a host of others.

Even when he took an old song he fused it to his own genius to make it immortal. Perhaps the best example is "A Red, Red Rose", where the old words:

> Her cheeks are like the Roses,
>   That blossoms fresh in June,
> O she's like a new-strung instrument
>   That's newly put in tune.

were turned to this:

> O my luve is like a red, red rose,
>   That's newly sprung in June,
> O my luve is like a melodie,
>   That's sweetly play'd in tune.

3

Burns means business in South-west Scotland

This was the craftsmanship of a shepherd whittling a beautiful crook from a plain ash bough, or the farm lad fashioning a beautiful harvest plait from a few straws in the cornfield. These original words, later in the song, were gey ordinary when Burns set to work on them:

> The seas they shall run dry,
>   And rocks melt into sands,
> Then I'll love you still my dear,
>   When all those things are done.

By his pen they were transformed:

> Till a' the seas gang dry, my dear,
>   And the rocks melt wi' the sun:
> And I will love thee still, my dear,
>   While the sands o' life shall run.

Clouds soon began to pass across the blue skies which had begun his stay at Ellisland. The first year his crop failed, the next promised little better. With another child born to Jean he applied for and was given an appointment with the Excise. Although Ellisland was successful poetically—producing "Tam O' Shanter" in addition to the many, many glorious songs—it was not a success as a farming venture, and Burns abandoned it after three and a half years to live in Dumfries, first at a house in what is now Bank Street, and then in Mill Street, now called Burns Street.

Time was running out; he was becoming an increasingly sick man. Many slanders were spoken by pious Victorians about these last years; they said he was drunken and unable to support his family. They were wrong—he was a sick man certainly, but not through any excess of drink or love. His heart was strained by overwork in his youth. Nor was Burns poor. He was well paid, and his excise work brought in far more than many a respectable man in Dumfries earned. His financial embarrassment at the time of his death was temporary, and was due to the reduction of imports because of the war with France.

However, in the early part of 1796 his health was deteriorating; rheumatic pains racked his wasting frame, and his doctors advised him to try sea-bathing at Brow on the Solway Firth. They might just as well have signed a death warrant there and then. Burns knew his life was in danger, Jean was expecting another child, and a small debt troubled him greatly. He wrote to his cousin for some money to tide him over; he wrote to Mrs. Dunlop to try to heal the breach with her, and he wrote to his father-in-law, appealing for Mrs. Armour to come to Jean's side urgently.

At the middle of July he returned home. All the countryside knew he was dying, and knots of people in the street passed on the latest news of his condition. By the 21st his heart was too tired to carry-on any longer, and Burns died. Dumfries gave him the best funeral it could, with military honours and a salvo fired over his grave. At that same moment Jean was in labour bearing another son.

What is it in Burns that appeals to the Scot and to the world? First and foremost his life story is a romantic one, filled with pathos. Here is the poor boy in Scotland's story who became a king. Of course, Burns was not the humble man many believe him to be; he was a tenant farmer's son, a good cut above the labourer or weaver, and he knew it. But when the nobility took him to their hearts and admired him as a plain, unlettered ploughman poet, he was clever enough to nurse the illusion along. The success of Burns's life is, of course, heightened by his death at the tragically early age of thirty-seven, when he still had so much to give us.

We admire also the man. Here is someone who could surpass us all at living and loving. Secretly the world admires a great lover, be he Errol Flynn or Robert Burns—in him they see what they themselves would like to be, but cannot. Burns, too, was proud of his prowess in that direction, and he embarked on his affairs with great gusto and looked back on them with boastfulness that some-times passed the bounds of good taste. When he seduced Elizabeth

Paton and paid penance for it, he lightly wrote that he meant to get his guinea's worth.

In his writings Burns expresses all that we feel. His very genius was in being a typical Scotsman—the mass of complexes which we all are. This was no ordinary poet who viewed his fellow men from Olympian heights. His thoughts were seldom original; they lacked logic, consistence and even reasonableness at times, but that is how real people are. Burns could write swingeing satire against wealth and privilege and then pen a letter appealing to a patron for help to secure a post.

He was honest and said what he felt, and naturally he felt differently according to his fortunes and his mood. That is how he is able to appeal to all the world—to the Christian, Humanist, Communist, Socialist, Republican, Monarchist, and Nationalist or any other *an* or *ist*. Who else is held in equal esteem in Russia and America alike?

Burns did not demolish Scotland's traditional institutions—he attacked their abuse. It was not the Kirk that he wanted to destroy, but its narrow hypocrites. No one who has read "The Cotter's Saturday Night" could believe Burns to be against religion; and equally no one who has read "Holy Willie's Prayer" could believe that he would ever condone cant.

Burns appeals to Scots especially because he says so clearly what they can only feel, and he says it in their own language and with a dash of sentimentality to which they are so partial. How this sort of thing appeals to the Scot:

>The heart's aye, the part aye,
>That makes us right or wrang.

Or the lines pleading for tolerance:

>Then gently scan your brother man,
>Still gentler sister woman;
>Tho' they may gang a kennin wrang
>To step aside is human.

One could go on quoting snatches which are still on every Scottish tongue, and which are likely to be so for many generations to come.

And that brings us to another reason for gratitude to Burns. His poetry has kept alive the Scottish language far more than any other influence. Often it is said that the old Scottish tongue is dying, and right enough it has taken a knock since the advent of Standard English on radio. But no one who has stood in Ayr's Sandgate, or listened to the workers scaling from the die-stamping or carpet works in the town can fear for the Scottish dialect in this generation at least. Burns captured for all time the speech of South-western Scotland.

He also put on paper places in this corner of Scotland that might have remained in obscurity—Tarbolton (Tarbowton to its in-dwellers) might have been passed unnoticed but for Burns; without him Kirkoswald's past of 'riot and swagger' might have been unknown; and even Alloway would have vanished into the maw of Ayr. Better known places like Dumfries, Kilmarnock, and Irvine have a lustre they could never have enjoyed but for Burns, and Ayrshire folk can be thankful that he said:

> We'll sing auld Coila's plains and fells,
> Her moors red-brown wi' heather bells,
> Her banks and braes, her dens and dells.

Burns has also brought to us across two centuries the people who lived in Scotland in the eighteenth century—men and women who lived in obscurity have had immortality thrust upon them. As we read of Burns's life, or enjoy his poetry we can see these people— Richard Brown, the sailor friend of Irvine days on a Sabbath walk with the poet; David Sillar, shy with the girls where Robert was so free; Mrs. Dunlop of Dunlop, chiding him for his republican sympathies; Jean placidly biding her time until he was ready to marry her; her father nursing his wrath to keep it warm; 'Daddy' Auld and 'Holy Willie' Fisher tut-tutting in the background; Poosie Nancy entertaining her jolly beggars; John Wilson cheating Death in Tarbolton; and so many more that it would be impossible to name them.

And yet, grateful as we are that Robert Burns has set his imprint on this corner of Scotland, we know that the converse is also true. Burns made the South-west, but the South-west and all the people who passed through it before, made Burns.

II

THE LIE OF THE LAND

FOUR counties lie within the frame of this portrait—Wigtown, Kirkcudbright, the western part of Dumfries, and most of Ayrshire. On the map the area looks like a great blunted arrowhead pointing across the North Channel towards Northern Ireland, which is less than twenty miles away. This triangular shape is deceptive, for it suggests a compact region similar in character throughout, and South-west Scotland is not like that at all—it comprises widely differing counties, each with its own typical scenery and character, and totally unlike its neighbour.

Ayrshire in the north is the only part which has been touched by the black fingers of industry, for it is the county with coal. Yet, Ayrshire also has some fine mixed and dairy-farming land, numerous private estates, and its towns are dormitories for business men who travel to Glasgow each day. Dumfries, apart from a little coal, which seems to have strayed over from Ayrshire, is a shire of rich red soil which yields well. It has little industry, and that all light. The farming lands of Dumfriesshire continue westward into the Stewartry of Kirkcudbright, but soon the contours become more twisted and dairy cows are displaced by sheep until one reaches the heart of Galloway, which is gnarled with mountains, scooped out with lochs, and is being filled with new forests which will supply timber to future generations. In Wigtown the mountains fall away to rich farmland, running all the way through the Machars and Rhinns of Galloway to the sea. Huge dairy farms and pretty little painted towns are a feature of the county.

That oversimplified sketch of the four counties shows what a cross-section of Scotland the South-west is. Here are found coal-fields equal to those of Lanarkshire or Fife, sandy shores like the Moray coast, sheer cliffs redolent of Aberdeenshire or Orkney, villages as picturesque as those in the East Neuk of Fife, and mountains and moors as wild as Sutherland. Such variety makes this a fascinating, self-sufficient corner of Scotland, but it also makes description difficult. Hillocky Kyle seems far from the glens of Galloway, the soggy Irvine coast is remote from the Solway sands, and the heather-clad peaty moors above the Rowantree School might be a thousand miles away from the subtropical gardens of Culzean Castle. And yet these places are all within the compass of a hundred miles, and often much less. Indeed, from one point on the Straiton to Newton Stewart road the hills to the west suddenly open out and the panorama encompasses the Stinchar valley, and Ailsa Craig which is on the doorstep of Culzean Castle.

Surface differences are due to differences in the rock formations that lie beneath the soil—rocks which were laid down over millions of years, making the country what it is long before man came on the scene.

Rocks and soil are our earliest history books. To the trained eye of the geologist they tell much about the making of the country. They indicate how the rocks were laid down, and the subsequent movements and influences which shaped them during the earth's early life. Where there is no obvious information to be found man can piece together more of the story from clues in the arrangement of the rocks or the fossils found in them. Just as the archaeologist can tell of past civilisations from the layers of rubble he exposes in his dig, the geologist—or rather the palaeontologist—can deduce much from the fossils of early life embedded in the layers of rock.

The most important group of rocks in this part of Scotland are called *sedimentary* because they were once sediment beneath the seas which covered the present day landmass. Over millions of years this sediment became compacted into hard rocks—the conglomerates, sandstones, and shales which lie below the soil. Of course the rocks did not stay in the neat layers in which they were laid down; they have been tilted by earth movements until they are closely folded over one another. And among them have appeared *igneous* rocks whose origins are volcanic, as they poured from the centre of the earth and hardened on the surface, or hardened underneath and were exposed as the softer sedimentary rocks above them were eroded away. Whatever their origin igneous rocks are not stratified like sedimentary ones; they are crystalline, and contain many minerals.

As if the convulsions under the earth's crust were not enough the surface has been further shaped by Ice Age glaciers, and by the workings of river, wind and rain over millions of years. These forces have rounded many of the mountain tops; they have made valleys, and they have scooped out glens and lochs.

We have spoken of folding of the rocks, but sometimes the convulsions did more. As pressures built up within the earth, the surface would often crack along a line of weakness, leaving a valley, or pushing rocks upwards on one side of the crack and downwards on the other. Several of these cracks can be seen on the map, for Scotland is scored by long faults running along a North-east-South-west axis. The Great Glen of Inverness-shire is one; the Highland Line from Stonehaven to Dumbarton is another; the southern edge of the Central Lowlands is a third, beginning at Dunbar and ending at Girvan.

The rocks of the South-west of Scotland are largely sedimentary, with intrusions of igneous rock in many places, and they range in age from north to south, with the youngest in the north. The centre of Ayrshire is composed of carboniferous rocks—a type which includes calciferous or yellow sandstone, carboniferous limestone, upper or mountain limestone, and of course, coal measures which had their origins probably 250 million years ago. To the east of Ayrshire old red sandstone is found in the hilly parts, and it runs intermittently along the edge of the southern uplands fault until Maybole where it forms a large triangle bounded on one side by the coast.

South of the fault lies the core of Galloway, a hard band of slaty Ordovician rock, which dates from some 400 million years ago. This follows the usual North-east to South-west trend and it extends right to the Solway shore at the top of Luce Bay, where another fault begins and runs (again North-eastwards) through Kirkcudbright and Dumfriesshire. South of this fault lie beds of Silurian rocks which are a continuation of those of the English Lake District. This Silurian rock extends to the Borders where it is overlaid by old red sandstone about Melrose. Throughout both the Ordovician and Silurian bands are found intrusions of igneous rocks and new red sandstone.

AYRSHIRE

The fault which marks the edge of the Central Lowlands runs through Southern Ayrshire, and to the south of it the scenery becomes rugged, with ranges of sombre hills marching far into Kirkcudbright. However, this does not mean that all of Ayrshire north of the fault is flat—on the contrary, it is only on reaching Ayr that one encounters anything that could be remotely classed as a plain. And even Kyle, which lies between the rivers Doon and Irvine, soon folds itself into more bumps than a badly tossed bed. Here the underlying rocks contain coal measures which were for long the economic heart of Ayrshire, bringing as a sort of trade mark great pyramids of slag—the bings, as they are called thereabouts—to mark the presence of each mine. The workings began at Glenburn, just behind Prestwick, and ran through Annbank, Tarbolton, and Auchinleck to Old and New Cumnock. Nowadays coalmining is no longer the vital industry it once was, and even where it is still carried on it does not deface the country as extensively as formerly; Killoch Colliery, on the road from

Ayr to Ochiltree, looks like a factory with twin, grey towers and
a long, glass-fronted building. Here the wheel no longer winds
wearily at the pithead and no great flat-topped bing has spread
across acres of farmland. There is smell, of course, and the burns
around the pit are polluted, but in mining even that is progress.
The coal seams turn south from the Cumnocks and are worked
along the Doon valley from Dalmellington, and again at Dailly
in the valley of The Water of Girvan.

Associated with the coal measures are deposits of iron ore, and it
was the juxtaposition of the two that made Central Ayrshire rich
industrially. However, the only ironworks left in the county is to
the north at Glengarnock.

Elsewhere in Britain one associates coalmining with drab towns
and lowering country, but not in Ayrshire. If it were not for
occasional bings, one would not know that mining was being
carried on. Yet, while some men are scooping out the black heart
of Ayrshire, others are cultivating its surface. The soil of Central
Ayrshire is heavy and rich, tending towards clay, and it is eminent-
ly suited to mixed farming and dairying. Farms are not usually
large, and from almost any point half a dozen farmsteads can be
seen on the brows of the hills or in the folds of valleys, easy to pick
out because of their bright red haysheds.

Towards the coast the soil lightens to sand, although in places,
especially south of Irvine, it also becomes wet and boggy. Nevertheless, this coast has been put to good use as a recreation centre
for Glaswegians, who flock on every good weekend to the
beautiful sandy beaches of Troon, Prestwick, and Ayr. The bents
beyond the beaches have been turned into some of the country's
finest golf courses, and Prestwick alone has three courses, Troon
has five, and Ayr two. Even the wet land between the mouths
of the Irvine and Garnock, was utilised for many years as a racecourse, aptly called Bogside, where the Scottish Grand National
was run each year. However, the demand for building land
became too great for Bogside Racecourse to survive, and it has
been sold for future industrial development.

Travelling inland from Ayr or Irvine woodland is scarce at first, and the land often has a shorn look, broken only by the brilliant-shaded thorn and beech hedges. Even on private estates, which are still numerous hereabouts, the woods have been thinned, and when estates have been bought by municipal or other public bodies, the first thought has been to sell off the timber as quickly as possible, and mutilate the countryside. One can only hope that the same authorities will replant, otherwise the country will lose one of its most precious and most beautiful natural assets.

Kyle is well watered by three rivers; the Irvine and Doon, which form its boundaries, and the Ayr which runs through the centre of the district. These rivers, with their tributary streams and burns (none of which aspire to the name of river), make for rich grazing land.

The river Irvine rises just over the county boundary in Lanarkshire, near the battlefield of Drumclog, and makes few digressions as it flows with determination through the lace-making towns of Darvel and Newmilns to Galston, Hurlford, and Kilmarnock. Only then does it begin to wind across the plain to Irvine, where it sweeps northwards, changes its mind, and turns south again to share the estuary of the river Garnock. In its upper waters, before Darvel the Irvine is joined by the Logan Water, and at Darvel by the Glen Water, either of which, from their size, might fairly claim to be the parent stream. Apart from a few burns there is no major tributary thereafter until Cessnock Water feeds in from the south. Cessnock Water begins in the foothills of Distinthill, and after flowing South-west it turns North-east, passing close to Mauchline and Mossgiel before it meets the Irvine between Galston and Hurlford. At Kilmarnock the Craufurdland Water and Fenwick Water unite to feed the Irvine, and last of all comes the Annick Water just before that final twist at the sea.

Industry shares the Irvine valley with agriculture. Lace-making is old established at Darvel, and Kilmarnock has added light industries to carpets, whisky and heavy engineering, its traditional manufactures. Irvine itself is again prospering after some years of decline. Two centuries ago when Burns went there to learn flax-dressing, Irvine was a major seaport. In due course it was ousted by Ardrossan, Troon, Ayr, and Glasgow, so that when I first knew Irvine thirty years ago it was lifeless and decayed. Now great expansion has come to its environs and the town has tidied itself up so that it is once again a place worthy of notice—a cheering thought this, for that sweep of river past the tall spire of the town kirk is potentially beautiful. Much has still to be done, but now it has been designated a new town for great expansion.

Like the Irvine, the river Ayr rises on the Lanarkshire border—at Glenbuck, and its beginnings are modest enough as it passes across the moorlands of Muirkirk which are high, open and extremely bleak. Here it is fed by the Garpel Water on its left bank, and the Greenock and Whitehaugh Waters on its right. Suddenly the Ayr becomes beautiful, and at times wild also, as it winds by Sorn and Catrine and—now augmented by the Lugar Water—Barskimming. This is the romantic river which Burns knew so well; it is where he bade farewell to Highland Mary; and it is scenery to inspire a poet, as the river wimples and turns—now gentle, now tumbling wild—through wooded glens, and past little green meadows in which cattle graze. The twistings bring the river to Stair and past Gadgirth, beyond which its last tributary of importance, the Water of Coyle, flows in. Like the Irvine, the Ayr has a final fling, turning north so that Annbank seems to be held tight within its folds, south again by Auchincruive, and then due west to Ayr and the sea. As it passes under the bridges of Ayr, the river is tidal and looks its best when the water is full. It flows first under the rebuilt Victoria Bridge, then under the railway and pedestrian bridges to pass behind the town's High Street as if it were ashamed to be seen. Then come the most famous of all Ayr's bridges—the Auld Brig and the New Brig, about which Burns wrote the poem, "The Brigs of Ayr". To be accurate the Auld Brig is the one about which the poem was written, but the new one is a rebuilt version of the one to which the Auld Brig boasted: "I'll be a brig when ye're a shapeless cairn."

The prophesy came true; the new bridge fell down in a storm in 1870. Just below the new bridge the river Ayr opens up into a fine harbour busy with fishing boats and cargo ships which take away coal and bring timber and other commodities vital to Ayrshire's life.

Burns made verse around the river Ayr; he did more to the Doon—he immortalised it, although those who view it only at Alloway miss the best of its course. The source of the river at Loch Doon is easy enough to reach by a good road, yet the only people who visit it are anglers and Ayr folk on a weekend outing or an early closing day run. A road runs right along the dog-leg shore of the loch and gives fine views of the water. On a gurley day when small rain beats into one's chilled marrow and the flat-topped hills are lost in mist, Loch Doon impresses; on a bright spring one it exhilarates. Few people live by Loch Doon now, but it has seen the making of some of Scotland's history. In Pictish times this must have been a place of some importance for nine hollowed-out oak canoes were found here in the early part of the last century. During the wars of Scotland's Independence both the English and the Scots used the castle which stood on an island in the middle of the loch as a stronghold, and it remained a fortress until James V sacked it in his bid to curb the power of his nobles.

From time to time man has raised and lowered the level of the loch to prevent flooding, to reclaim land, for a madcap scheme to build a seaplane base on the loch during the 1914–18 War, and most recently as part of southern Scotland's hydro-electric scheme. The final raising of the loch in the 1930s threatened to submerge the ruins of the castle, and so the walls were carefully dismantled and re-erected on the Ayrshire bank.

A dam encloses Loch Doon so that the river begins its course from sluice gates which may control the quantity of water, but not the manner in which it flows. Here the water cascades through the narrow, picturesque gorge of Ness Glen, making its first mile perhaps the loveliest of its course. The river continues past Dalmellington and the half-demolished remains of Waterside village and its giant slag bing, to Patna, which once stood off the main road on the far bank of the river. Patna's council and prefabricated houses now span the Doon and spill far beyond the main road. Here the land is low and soggy, and subject to such flooding when the Doon runs wild that local people have nicknamed the watery soil, the Promised Land.

Fed by many burns the Doon now begins to wind as it reaches the edge of the Ayrshire plain. It passes Hollybush House and Skeldon, where blankets were once made and sent round the world bearing the label 'Made by ye banks and braes o' bonnie Doon'. Looping past Dalrymple it reaches Cassillis, where it is still very much as Burns described it:

> Amang the bonie winding banks,
> Where Doon rins, wimplin' clear. . . .

This is the northern march of Kennedy country, for Cassillis was one of the strongholds of this family which reigned from Ayr to the Solway. As the boundary of their land the Doon was the scene of much fighting among Kennedys, Mures and Crawfords, which delayed progress in South-west Scotland for centuries, and inspired novels by Sir Walter Scott and Galloway novelist, S. R. Crockett.

However, the Doon is peaceful these days as it passes a series of beautiful houses—Monkwood, Auchendrane, Nether Auchendrane and Doonholm—all of them privately owned except Nether Auchendrane, a home for the elderly of Ayrshire. The Doon has now reached Alloway, where it flows under the hunchback bridge which Tam O'Shanter crossed to escape from the witches, passes behind the Auld Kirk, and continues to Doonfoot and the sea.

Its estuary is no more than a couple of miles from that of the River Ayr.

CARRICK

Within a mile or two of Ayr Carrick begins, for the river Doon is its boundary; within a mile or two of Ayr the plain of Kyle ends also. From Alloway the road south rises quickly, and soon

Kyle lies spread out far to the north and east. The hill along whose shoulder the road runs is Newarkhill the northermost bluff of the Carrick hills, a long range of low green summits and moors stretching from Newarkhill through Brown Carrick Hill and Mochrum, to the hills above Dailly and the valley of the Water of Girvan. Highways south from Ayr follow one side or the other of these hills—one by the coast and two inland. The coast road passes Butlin's Holiday Camp and the sandstone Heads of Ayr, which jut into the Firth of Clyde, before it continues to Dunure, Croy Brae and Culzean Castle. The contours hereabouts are deceptive; Croy Brae is a hill which isn't. Visitors come from miles around to test the phenomenon of being able to freewheel up it, but having to use power to descend it. The explanation of this piece of sleight of hand on nature's part, is that the road is formed on sidelong ground with the western half on the surface of the ground and the eastern half in cutting. Beyond the cutting lies a mass of wood and beyond that Knoweside Hill. The combined effect of these four features creates the impression that you are descending towards Croy Glen when you are actually rising. Continue half a mile along the road and look back at the entire sweep of the brae, and the explanation becomes clear. Croy Brae has another name—the Electric Brae—because it was once thought that electrical or magnetic attraction caused the phenomenon, but that has long since been discounted. Nevertheless, the name persists.

The other two roads run inland and unite at Maybole; the High Road by Culroy is well up on the hillside, while the Low Road by Minishant follows the valley floor. Both follow the Doon for five miles, and then continue over a low plateau until they enter the Girvan valley. Before Maybole the valley widens into a broad plain stretching through the villages of Kirkmichael and Crosshill to the Straiton hills. From Maybole, an attractive old town set on the steep slope, the patchwork of little fields that make up this plain is spread out prettily, and farms are strung across the landscape. In the distance the hills of Galloway stand out blue on a clear day, but when rain comes they vanish into a pall of mist.

Ayr—Tam O' Shanter Inn, now a museum

On the seaward side the hills dip steeply to the Firth, leaving room for no more than a string of fine dairy and early potato farms all the way to Girvan. Proof of the mild climate which this coast enjoys can be found in the gardens of Culzean Castle where tropical plants grow in the open air and flowers bloom earlier in the year than elsewhere.

At Girvan the scene changes again. Hitherto the hills have been low, but now the land rises quickly although the peaks are still no more than a thousand feet high until the Stinchar valley is crossed and the countryside becomes brown instead of green. The hills rise to the range which runs through Shalloch on Minnoch, Kirriereoch, and over the county boundary into Kirkcudbright, where the Merrick stands higher than any other peak in the whole of South Scotland. Here all the hills are over two thousand feet—Shalloch on Minnoch is 2,520 feet; Kirriereoch, 2,562 feet; and the Merrick, 2,764 feet.

South of Girvan the hills push out to the coast so that the road is forced in places to cling precariously to the rocks as it goes through Kennedy's Pass and past the Bannane Head.

Just off the road white-crowned waves break over black rocks and dare one to leave the high road. Over the crest of the hills upland farms stretch to the Stinchar valley, and then the country is given over to sheep and forest.

South of Ballantrae, the land rises, but soon falls away again into the narrow valley of the Water of App, a short glen which resembles a Highland one more than a Lowland one. Just beyond Glenapp the Galloway Burn marks the boundary of Ayrshire.

AILSA CRAIG

All over South Scotland great granite blocks intrude among the sedimentary rocks, but none more prominently than Ailsa Craig. When Sir William Brewster travelled through Ayrshire in the summer of 1635 he noted that "This rock on the island was in our view three days whilst we travelled betwixt sixty and seventy

4

Prestwick International Airport booking hall
Trees enhance Kyle's beauty

miles, and when you are at a great distance, it presents itself in shape like a sugar loaf; and when you approach nearer, it seems lower and flatter at the top, but it is a much-to-be-admired piece of the Lord's workmanship."

Sugar loaf-shaped is a fair description, but Ailsa Craig has others. How about calling it a battered bowler hat? Or even Paddy's Milestone because it looks like a weather-worn milestone on the sea route from the Clyde to Ireland? Whatever way you see it, Ailsa Craig cannot be missed by the traveller on shore or by sea, since it rises sheer from the water nine and a half miles off Girvan. It looks so perfectly symmetrical when viewed from the distance that it seems to have been patted carefully into shape and, although under a mile in diameter, it rises, 1,114 feet above the Firth.

Geologically Ailsa Craig is noteworthy too. It is formed of a fine-grained granite rare enough to have its own name, Ailsite, and capable of taking on such a polish that it is put to an unusual use—the making of curling stones. A century ago fifty pairs of stones were fashioned from Ailsa's greyish-green granite each year. By the turn of the century the output was a thousand pairs, but today four thousand pairs of stones are quarried each year, and they are thrown in matches and bonspiels in many parts of the world, but especially in Canada, which has taken the 'roaring game' as its own, and in the United States.

Ailsa Craig can still be visited in the summer, by a little boat from Girvan, but otherwise it is abandoned to the lighthouse-keepers and seabirds. Gannets, puffins, guillemots, razorbills, kittiwakes and gulls clamour on its summit, nest on its granite ledges, and fish off its shores. In the Middle Ages they were a delicacy for the table of the Abbots of Crossraguel Abbey, and until recent times they were fair game for anyone with a gun or even a stick as the Rev. Roderick Lawson, Minister of Maybole, testified in a charming little book he compiled about Ailsa Craig towards the end of the last century. Puffins were so plentiful then that a former tenant on the island once undertook to kill eighty dozen with a pole in a single day; he succeeded, and a former owner of my copy of Lawson's book was prompted to add the marginal cry: "The brute!" Today, the birds live under the wing of the Law, safe from Abbot's cook and murdering islander.

DUMFRIESSHIRE

Dumfriesshire lays fair claim to a share of the Burns legend; he lived in the valley of the Nith during the years which produced some of his best poetry and almost all of his best songs, and he died in Dumfries. It is impossible to measure the precise inspiration that Nithsdale was to him, but there can be no doubt that his head was full of poetry as he journeyed along the Nith to visit Jean at Mossgiel, while the farmhouse at Ellisland was being built. And it must equally have been full of poetry, probably of a more sombre kind, as he returned to Ellisland.

Nithsdale is capable of inspiring the least poetic. Whereas other rivers conform to the rules and begin as narrow mountain streams, flow through a gradually widening valley and then open into a plain towards the sea, the Nith is a rebel. At times its valley is wide, at others narrow, and nearly always it is beautiful.

The river rises in Ayrshire midway between New Cumnock and Dalmellington in the range dominated by Enoch Hill. First it flows north and west, but at New Cumnock, where the Afton Water joins it, the river makes a sweep to the east and then settles on a southerly course. At Cumnock too, the river is joined by the main road and railway to Dumfries and the English border, both of which follow it all the way to Dumfries. At first as the Ayrshire county boundary is crossed the road seems to have a precarious foothold, running above and apart from both river and railway, and seeming, from the driver's seat of a car, to be thrust aside rudely at every dip in the hills. The high moorland country that has run through eastern Ayrshire continues across the county border, and apart from a sign at the side of the road there is nothing to tell that this is another county. Even coal-mining continues into Dumfriesshire, although it is a dying industry, and local folk are alarmed that nothing is following on to take its place. Kirkconnel, has the same look of solid decay as the Cumnocks, and its appearance is marred by a vast township of prefabricated houses which though built to last ten years, are still occupied after twice as long. It seems a pity that a potentially pleasant place should be so spoilt.

From Ayr, farming and coal-mining have gone together, but now the mining vanishes. Sanquhar, which has been a mining area for eight hundred years, no longer has a single pit, but it remains an attractive place which has no intention of dying yet. Here the valley opens out and the soil becomes rich and red. Marginal land supporting sheep and fat cattle is left behind, and now there are dairy farms, down Nithsdale to Dumfries, and westward through Moniaive. At Sanquhar the valley opens majestically but soon it narrows again, and is filled with beautiful woods as the road winds down to Drumlanrig Castle, the seat of the Dukes of Buccleuch, and Thornhill.

Thornhill takes one's breath away—here in Southern Scotland is a boulevard sweeping proudly past the solid sandstone houses and shops of the village. And in keeping with the continental atmosphere of the wide, tree-lined street, the Drumlanrig Café stands in the centre of the village with brilliant polka-dot umbrellas sheltering its tables from the sun. Now there's optimism for you—sun-umbrellas in rainy South-west Scotland. However, if the sun is absent one has a better excuse for entering the Ali Baba's cave of sweets that lies within.

South of Thornhill the Nith valley widens again, and the river waters fine farming country past Auldgirth Bridge and into the part of Dumfriesshire most closely linked with Burns. Here is Ellisland; the byres, barn and farmhouse set neatly round its farmyard, and every building whitewashed and with painted lintels. Suddenly you realise that this scene has scarcely changed in two hundred years, and here is a clue to the secret of the continuing appeal of Burns. We are still essentially the same people as lived here at the end of the eighteenth century, so as Burns was writing for his contemporaries, he wrote for us also.

Ellisland is set beside the river, and one can walk along the riverside path where Burns wrote "Tam O'Shanter", seeking inspiration in the stony waters of the Nith. The interior of the farmhouse is little altered. A room has been set aside for visitors, and a bathroom added by cutting a slice off the original kitchen. But changes have been slight, and even the original kitchen ham cleeks or hooks still hang from the ceiling in the bathroom.

Across the shallow river lies Dalswinton, the farm which the experts say Burns would have been better advised to have taken in preference to Ellisland. Dalswinton has its claim to fame, too, for it was on the loch there that Patrick Miller (who owned both farms and rented Ellisland to Burns), tried out his invention, a steam-powered boat, in 1788. It is gratifying to know from the Dumfries Journal of the day that "It answered Mr. Miller's expectations fully, and afforded great pleasure to the spectators present".

Dumfries is only a few miles away, and there the Burns Country ends, for it was in Dumfries that Burns died. The town cherishes its links with the poet, and it is difficult to escape from his influence. The house where he died is carefully preserved, although most of its neighbours are gone; the Globe Inn where he caroused still dispenses liquor and jollity; and St. Michael's Church by which Robert, Jean and five of their children are buried, still calls the townsfolk every Sabbath morning. As if this were not enough they have put up a statue to the poet at the top of the High Street.

Dumfries is the Queen of the South and, although part of the town most closely connected with Burns is sadly decayed, it is a prosperous and attractive town. It was once a considerable seaport from which thousands of Scots set out for new lives in the New World, but those days are gone, and today it is now a market town with its life centred round its market and industries connected with agriculture. That is not to say that it has no other life

—plastics for packaging, hosiery, gloves and rubber products are also produced, and it is always seeking new industries.

Across the Nith and now part of Dumfries, lies Maxwelltown, with new housing estates and the ruins of Lincluden Abbey. But the Nith is the county boundary and this is Galloway, which may have scant connection with Burns, but it has its own sons of note. If we are out of the Burns Country we are in the Paul Jones Country, the S. R. Crockett Country, and the Land of St. Ninian who brought Christianity to Scotland a century before St. Columba.

III

GALLOWAY—CRADLE OF SCOTLAND

BURNS had remarkably little connection with Galloway, despite
the fact that he lived so close to it and his excise work took him
along the Solway Coast. It is not really surprising though that he
did not write about it, for in the eighteenth century Galloway was
a remote place where the Gaelic tongue was just disappearing, and
in any case Sir Walter Scott and the romantic poets had not
awakened Scots to the beauty of their country.

However, Galloway does claim some Burns links, albeit slender
ones. At the Murray Arms Hotel, Gatehouse-of-Fleet, they will
show you the room where he wrote down "Scots Wha Hae", and
elsewhere in his poems and songs there are glancing references to
other parts of Galloway. He must have had some knowledge of
the bleak heart of the province to write:

> Behind yon hills where Stinchar flows,
>   'Mang moors an' mosses many, O,
> The wintry sun the day has clos'd,
>   And I'll awa' tae Nanie O.

His Selkirk Grace referred, not to the town of Selkirk, but to
the Earl of Selkirk who lived at Kirkcudbright, and he also wrote
of the winding banks of Cree. But when he came to Kirkmaiden
he had to take liberties with the name to preserve the rules of
poetry:

Hear, Land o' Cakes, and Brither Scots
Frae Maidenkirk to Johny' Groats.

Galloway can get along quite well without Burns, for it has its
own sons and daughters of whom it is proud. This is the land of
S. R. Crockett, Paul Jones, St. Ninian, Devorgilla, William
Wallace and Robert the Bruce and the brave things they did for
Scotland. The great battles of Scotland's War of Independence
may belong to Falkirk, Stirling and Bannockburn, but it was
among the Galloway hills that the English were harried and held
at bay. For proof take the road up the side of Loch Trool until
you come to the great rock set high above the loch and bearing the
inscription:

IN LOYAL REMEMBERANCE
OF ROBERT THE BRUCE
KING OF SCOTS
WHOSE VICTORY IN THIS
GLEN OVER AN ENGLISH
FORCE IN MARCH, 1307,
OPENED THE CAMPAIGN OF
INDEPENDENCE WHICH HE
BROUGHT TO A DECISIVE
CLOSE AT BANNOCKBURN
ON THE 24TH JUNE, 1314.

Looking across the hills which encompass the loch, one's heart
stirs to the realisation that this is the cradle of Scotland's independence, and the least nationalistic Scot must warm to Bruce and his
victories.

Galloway runs between 'the braes o' Glenapp' and the 'Brig
en' O' Dumfries', and it comprises Scotland's two most South-
westerly counties, Wigtown and Kirkcudbright. I say the counties
of Wigtown and Kirkcudbright, but that is not strictly correct,
for one should say the county of Wigtown and the Stewartry of
Kirkcudbright. The name refers to the time when the king was

represented by a Steward who collected the royal revenues, and, although there were a number of Stewartries in Scotland, this is the only one that has survived. The most famous of Kirkcudbright's Stewards was Walter, who married Marjorie, daughter of Robert the Bruce, and founded the Scottish Royal House of Stewart. The province runs from the wild mountains where Bruce hid and fought, to the Solway Firth, where saintly Ninian built his church and prayed. It contrasts mighty mountains and lochs with sweet pastures; it ranges from moors which support only sheep and trees to lush pasture land flowing with milk and Galloway honey.

The aspect of Galloway is southerly, for the land falls away to the south and is watered by a succession of rivers which flow from the high moors through gentle pastures to the Solway Firth. From right to left on the map, these rivers are the Nith, Urr, Dee, Tarff, Fleet, Cree, Bladnoch and Luce, every one rivalling the others for the title of the most beautiful.

What strikes the stranger about Galloway? Well, first there is beauty unsurpassed in Scotland, even if the scenery is not on the grand scale of the Highlands. Then there is the peace, for this place does not know what over-crowding or urgency mean. Galloway is a relaxing place, with contented people, who have time to enjoy life and to enjoy each other's company. Only a few days ago in a shop in Port William it took me fifteen minutes to buy some sweets, because so many varieties had to be offered and every time the deal was on the point of being clinched, the kindly shopkeeper remembered another variety which she had not yet shown me.

In another shop—in Glen Trool village this time—I contrasted the purchase of a birthday card with the battle in those London card-shops which are at present so plentiful and so crowded. The card was incidental to the social occasion in Glen Trool.

"Ane o' my lambs wis deid this mornin'," the customer remarked, removing her reading glasses and abandoning the selection of a card momentarily.

"Och, Och, and them daeing that weel," the shopkeeper sympathised. "D'ye ken whit wis wrang wi'it?"

"Aye, it wis deid."

There the conversation died also, but it was followed by several others before the card was chosen and the customer delved into her purse for some money. She was a few coppers short, so she gave the shopkeeper what she had with the explanation: "Och, weel, Duncan, I'll gie ye the rest o' the money the nicht—an' then I'll tak' it off ye at nap."

The moral is plain. The Galloway folk may have their kindliness and pawkiness, but they are shrewd enough underneath. If you do not believe that, visit Newton Stewart on any market day.

The whole of Galloway lies south of the fault which divides the Central Lowlands from the Southern Uplands, and its central core is that belt of slaty Ordovician rock which runs from the Wigtown coast through the Merrick and Kells ranges of upper Kirkcudbright to the Lowther, Moorfoot and Lammermoor Hills. On the Wigtown coast, where it stretches from Glenapp to Portpatrick, this band is fifteen miles wide, but throughout its course it varies between that and five miles. Apart from the coastal strip the rest of the province comprises the belt of Silurian rocks, beginning between Portpatrick and the Mull of Galloway, and running eastwards until it becomes overlaid with old red sandstone near Melrose.

Throughout both formations other rocks have intruded. First there are other sedimentary rocks, like the new red sandstone around Dumfries, on the Solway and behind Stranraer—rocks which have been used much for building and have given many of the little towns of South-west Scotland their dark red, comfortable look. More prominent, however, are the igneous intrusions— the granite masses which have been exposed by the erosion and movement of softer rocks above them, and which now form the hard, cold face of Galloway, with bogs and lochs as its principal features. The largest of these is actually on the Solway Firth—the Criffel, around Dalbeattie which covers seventy-five square miles.

The next two in size are Cairnsmore of Fleet, where the granite extends to fifty-seven square miles, and a forty-seven square mile rectangle south of Loch Doon. Inland, there is a smaller patch of granite at Cairnsmore of Carsphairn, and on the coast it emerges at Creetown, Crammag Head and the Mull of Galloway.

KIRKCUDBRIGHT

The wildest part of upper Galloway, is the border between the counties of Ayr and Kirkcudbright—indeed, the Merrick range marches right out of Ayrshire into Kirkcudbright, with Shalloch-on-Minnoch in Ayr and the Merrick itself in Kirkcudbright. The county boundary runs through Kirriereoch, the third main peak of the range, along the eastern shore of Loch Doon, and north of Cairnsmore of Carsphairn to Windy Standard peak.

Galloway is fortunate for much of its high moorland has been or is being planted with forests, and these forests have been turned into a place for recreation for climbers, hill-walkers, naturalists, and tourists who simply want to enjoy the scenery. This is Glen Trool Forest Park which extends almost from Straiton in Ayrshire to Newton Stewart, covering 130,000 acres and taking in seven forests—Glen Trool, Carrick, Changue, Dundeugh, the Garraries and Kirroughtree. Within the forest lie the highest peaks of South Scotland, as well as numerous lochs and valleys, all within easy reach of the industrial centres of Ayrshire and Lanarkshire. A growing number of Englishmen, too, are finding their way here for it is an easy drive from Lancashire, and much less crowded than the Lake District. On an English holiday these twentieth-century border reivers swarm over from Carlisle, and to be fair to the Galloway folk they are welcomed peaceably and warmly.

If you drive into Galloway from Maybole by the road which goes through the Nick of the Balloch Pass, you will be able to see why the Merrick hills are also called the Awful Hand. From that road the four peaks of Tarfessock, Kirriereoch, the Merrick and Benyellary stand out like great knuckles with the Bennan further south as the thumb. From the Merrick peaks you can look across the boulder-strewn, loch-pitted country that is the Loch Doon granite mass. This is the Cauldron, lying enclosed by the Merrick and Rhinns of Kells ranges—bare, bleak country, incredibly carved by ice so that the lochs look ragged and unfinished. The lochs have splendid-sounding names—Recawr, Macaterick, Enoch, Neldricken, Valley, Dee, the Long and Round Lochs of the Dungeon and Long and Round Lochs of Glenhead. From the lochs numerous burns tumble across the bare granite towards Loch Doon. These burns, or lanes, as they are often called, are the true headwaters of the River Doon.

The Merrick range and the Cauldron end at Loch Trool, the most famous loch of Southern Scotland, and the gem of Galloway. The loch is not large—only a mile and a half long and half a mile across—but, it is very impressive as high, dark hills rise steeply from its shore. Standing by the Bruce Stone high above the loch, one looks across Mulldonach, down whose slopes the Scottish soldiers rolled great boulders onto the English army in 1307, to the higher peaks of Lamachan, Larg and Curleywee Hills, all of which are over two thousand feet.

Nature tries hard to impress in Galloway, but man has done great things also. On the eastern edge of the Lamachan Hills the Black Water of Dee has been dammed to form a broad loch called Clatteringshaws Loch, from which the water is led through a three-and-a-half-mile tunnel to a steep pipeline down the hillside into Glenlee Power Station, where it generates electricity. Glenlee is one of the power stations in the South of Scotland Electricity Board's Galloway hydro-electric scheme—a water-power scheme which was operating long before the Highlands ones were begun. The Galloway scheme was conceived in 1923, to harness the waters of the Dee and Doon basins, and the building of the scheme took place between 1931 and 1935. There are five power stations in series on the rivers Ken and Dee, with three reservoirs, Loch Doon, Clatteringshaws and Loch Ken, and the water is used several times to generate power. Loch Doon water is used four

times as it passes down the valley, and the water from Clatteringshaws, after being put to use at Glenlee, continues to Tongland
Power Station on the estuary of the river Dee.

A dam on Loch Doon gathers water which is piped into
Carsphairn Lane and other burns to feed Kendoon Reservoir from
which it passes through the three power stations of Kendoon,
Carsfad and Earlston, each of which has its own reservoirs and
dams. South of New Galloway Loch Ken forms the next reservoir, with Glenlochan Barrage at its southern end, and Tongland
Reservoir continues to gather the water for the last power station
at Tongland, just above Kirkcudbright.

Fortunately, the Galloway hydro-electric scheme has been conceived with care, and even the dams and five great concrete and
glass 'electricity factories' do not mar the scenic beauty of the area.
Indeed, as in Glen Trool Forest Park, trees have been planted, lochs
have been stocked with fish, and roads have been improved so
that the public can enjoy the amenities more fully. Loch Ken is a
tree-fringed strip of silver water, nowhere very wide, which is one
of the loveliest lochs in South Scotland, and the villages and towns
of New Galloway, Dalry and Castle Douglas remain unspoilt.
In Galloway no one can say that power has corrupted.

East of Loch Ken the scenery is less dramatic than the Merrick
or Rhinns. Nonetheless, it is beautiful, drunken landscape, rolling
through tiny hamlets with long names like Balmaclellan, Kirkpatrick Durham and Crocketford, to the Nith valley. Hills here
are never more than a thousand feet, and they are softly rounded
and greener than any on the other side at Loch Ken. At first this is
sheep-farming country, but dairy cows replace the sheep as the
bumps iron themselves out and one nears the 'Brig en' of
Dumfries' and the Burns Country again.

THE COAST

The Scots love to put evocative catchnames on places, and
the Kirkcudbright coast is no exception—between Dumfries

and Kirkcudbright town lies the *Paul Jones Country*; then the town of Kirkcudbright is the *Artists' Paradise*; and the road between Gatehouse-of-Fleet and Creetown is the *Most Beautiful Road*.

Paul Jones is better known (and better liked) in America than in Great Britain. On the other side of the Atlantic he is a hero, but to us he is a pirate, whose exploits along the Solway had all the hallmarks of punching one's old father on the nose—very undignified and not at all gentlemanly. Perhaps that is why the Scots are so reluctant to signpost the road to Arbigland in the parish of Kirkbean, where he was born in 1747. Certainly it has been left to the Americans to put up a plaque to mark the fact. At any rate John Paul (for that was his name until he added Jones after one of his benefactors) was born here, a gardener's son, and he left Scotland after an escapade in which he was jailed in Kirkcudbright Tolbooth on a charge of murder on the high seas. He returned to Europe during the War of American Independence, and brazenly sailed up the Solway to St. Mary's Isle, close to the Tolbooth where he had been imprisoned, and attempted to kidnap the Earl of Selkirk. Fortunately the Earl was away from home, and Paul Jones had to be content with his silver plate.

From Dumfries the road to Arbigland passes through New Abbey, a lovely village with the ruins of one of Galloway's three medieval abbeys. The rose-coloured ruins are all that remain of Sweetheart Abbey, which Devorgilla built in 1273, in memory of her husband, John Balliol, founder of Balliol College in Oxford and father of John Balliol, whom Robert the Bruce pushed off the Scottish throne. When Balliol died Devorgilla carried his embalmed heart in a silver casket for the rest of her life, and so the monks named her abbey *Dulce Cora*, which means Sweetheart.

From Sweetheart Abbey the road skirts the granite mass of the Criffel, through land which is peaceful and picturesque, despite its links with the rumbustious Paul Jones. The rough indentations of the mouth of the River Urr are set with the holiday villages of Rockcliffe and Kippford, now a great yachting centre. These villages are a preview of the beauties that lie further along the coast, after the road turns inland to cross the Urr near Dalbeattie, and then turns south to the second of the Galloway abbeys— Dundrennan, whose high walls stand proudly erect after so many centuries. Dundrennan was founded by David I and Fergus, Lord of Galloway, in 1142, and after four centuries it became a Protestant Kirk which it remained until the eighteenth century. Mary Queen of Scots spent her last night in Scotland at Dundrennan, and from there she crossed the Solway to imprisonment, trial and execution at Fotheringay.

A few miles beyond Dundrennan nature has taken another large bite out of the Solway—this time to form the estuary of the rivers Tarff and Dee, and at the head of this estuary is situated the county town of Kirkcudbright. Kirkcudbright is a great centre for arts and crafts in Southern Scotland, and it has a flourishing colony of artists living and working in it. The man responsible for the foundation of Kirkcudbright as an arts centre is, E. A. Hornel, who gave his home, beautiful eighteenth-century Broughton House to the town. It is now a museum. Hornel led the way, and others followed to restore the decaying seventeenth-century houses and turn the town into a showplace. Sculptors, potters and weavers have also contributed to this artists' paradise, and it is not surprising that the town has cast its spell over them all. Kirkcudbright, which was a busy seaport two centuries ago, lies at the mouth of the Dee, its painted houses crowned by the ruin of Maclellan's Castle, which Sir Thomas Maclellan of Bombie, a provost of the burgh, had built for himself in the sixteenth century. The town itself is beautiful, but so also is the verdant, farm-dotted countryside, and the coast has been carved by the centuries into coves and rocky promontories.

The road from Gatehouse-of-Fleet to Creetown is said to be the most beautiful road in Scotland, and Thomas Carlyle is reputed to have given it that title. It is said that once when he met Queen Victoria at Dean Stanley's house he was praising the beauty of Galloway in general and of the coast road in particular, and became so absorbed in the subject that "in drawing his chair closer to the Queen, he at last became aware he had fixed it on her dress, and that she could not move till he had withdrawn it".

Actually, the Gatehouse coast road was given its title long before Carlyle and the Queen met—John M'Diarmid, editor of the *Dumfries and Galloway Courier*, wrote in his *Sketchbook*, which was published in the 1830s, that this was probably the most beautiful shore road in the whole of Scotland. Galloway folk have dropped the word probably.

This road deserves its name—it skirts Wigtown Bay, passing Cardoness Castle, Dick Hatterick's Cave and Carsluith Castle. Woods and hills lie inland, and the road is edged with cottages whose gardens are filled with summer flowers which brighten even the dullest day. Alas, the beauty is spoiled by caravans, the felling of trees, and road works.

At the head of Wigtown Bay the estuary of the River Cree marks the county boundary, and as you cross the five dark spans that bridge the river you pass from sleepy Minnigaff in Kirkcudbrightshire to lively Newton Stewart in Wigtownshire.

WIGTOWNSHIRE

Wigtownshire is the gentle part of Galloway, with none of the dramatic hills or shapeless lochs, but in its quiet way the county pleases. It is a gentle county, as is fitting for the place where Christianity was born in Scotland, and Ninian's saintly hand still seems to be laid on it after sixteen centuries.

Like Gaul, Wigtownshire is divided into three parts—the Moors, which form the main mass of the county, the Machars, which are the great promontory on which the town of Wigtown is situated, and the Rhinns, that huge coathook peninsula bounded by Loch Ryan, Luce Bay and the North Channel.

THE MOORS

Like the rest of Galloway the Moors slope towards the south, until they reach the top of Luce Bay and Wigtown Bay. The name

The road to Willie's Mill, Tarbolton
Lochlie, Burns's home for four years

is apt, for none of the hills is more than a thousand feet above sea level, and more often they are nearer seven or eight hundred feet. In the north it is a bare, wild landscape, criss-crossed by burns and hill roads, and with brown of the peat and grey of the rock showing among the grass. Inland lie lochs Mabery, Dornal, Ochiltree and Penwhirn Reservoir, like great lumps of pewter among the dark hues of the country. On the coast, where the road from Ballantrae follows the edge of Loch Ryan, the land falls quickly to the water's edge. Here is another of those Government-sponsored white elephants, which mar the country and result in misery. Cairnryan was once a pretty village by the loch until the war came and a huge deep-water harbour was built there.

All was well, and one accepted the cranes and high wire fences, but with the end of the war the harbour became redundant and abandoned. Eventually the War Office sold the harbour to a private firm, leaving the village spoilt and the surrounding area with a huge unemployment problem. For years cranes stood at Cairnryan and a huge fence ran between the village and the loch. It seems a pity that no law forces Governments to restore what they have destroyed. Compared with the cost of building the harbour, its removal would have been cheap and worthwhile.

Stranraer spreads itself round the head of Loch Ryan, and its chief claim to fame is as the port for the short sea crossing to Ireland. Indeed, the whole town's life seems to be tied up with the ferry-service which runs to Larne, and there is even much Irish in the voices of the Stranraer people—we from the flatter Scottish vocal plains of Ayrshire call it Galloway-Irish. Except for its Old Castle where Claverhouse is said to have stayed in 1682, Stranraer has no ancient buildings. Indeed, the most fascinating building in the town is the North-west Castle, built by Sir John Ross, the man who discovered the North-west Passage, to look like a ship. It has now been turned into an hotel.

The two rivers flow south across the Moors—the Water of Luce, which cuts through the middle of the county and the Cree which forms the county boundary.

5

The river Nith at Ellisland

The Luce has two main streams—the Main Water of Luce and the Cross Water at Luce—both rising on the Ayrshire border, and uniting at New Luce Village. The valley opens out to rounded hills set among trees, and rolling pasture land where belted Galloway cattle and dairy cows graze. The river continues past the ruins of Glenluce, the third of the Galloway abbeys. Glenluce dates back nearly eight hundred years, and although it was pillaged for its building stone between the Reformation and this century, it is now in the care of the Ministry of Works, much restored and its surroundings wellkempt. Set back a little from the river is the village of Glenluce, and here the railway line and road from Newton Stewart, cross the river together before the river runs its last mile into Luce Bay.

The Cree begins life from Loch Moan as the boundary between Ayrshire and Kirkcudbright, and it is only at a point above Loch Ochiltree that it leaves Ayrshire and becomes the march between Wigtownshire and Kirkcudbright.

The river is joined by the Water of Minnoch which rises further north than the sources of the Cree, but even with this and innumerable burns from the mountains the Cree is neither wide nor deep. Except in winter or time of summer flood, it runs shallow with stones peering from the water like curious fish, passing through pleasant arable farmland, well filled with trees. The river is accompanied by a road which is banked with bluebells in the early summer. Penninghame in this broad, open valley has been chosen for Scotland's first open prison, and nowhere could suggest freedom better.

At Minnigaff, the Penkill Burn flows into the Cree just before the river passes sedately under the old bridge, which links Minnigaff and Newton Stewart, and then tumbles noisily over the weir which lies downstream. The townships on either side of the Cree have reversed their original positions—Minnigaff was once a bustling place when Newton Stewart was nothing, but now it is the other way round. Minnigaff is as peaceful a village as Newton Stewart is a bustling market town and woollen manufacturing centre. Newton Stewart is also a popular holiday town, especially for fishermen, and if you visit the Galloway Arms or any of the other fine little hotels in the town you can sample the Cree salmon which is smaller and sweeter-tasting than any you will ever taste in Scotland.

Newton Stewart is almost the end of the Cree—for a mile or two more it performs great, winding loops until the last tributary —the Palnure Burn—joins it, and the Cree issues into Wigtown Bay.

THE MACHARS

St. Columba usually gets the credit for introducing Christianity into Scotland when he sailed from Ireland to Iona in A.D. 563. Even Scots forget that more than a century earlier a man called Ninian built the first stone church in Scotland near the tip of the tapering peninsula which juts into the Solway Firth below Newton Stewart. Ninian was born beside the Solway about A.D. 360, the son of a British prince and, after studying in Rome, he returned home to build his church, which the Romans called *Candida Casa* —the White House. From the Anglo-Saxon version of Candida Casa is derived the name Whithorn. For such a small town Whithorn has a wide main street because in medieval times Scottish kings made pilgrimages to St. Ninian's shrine, and even today the priory is approached through an archway over which is set the royal arms of Scotland. The Reformation Parliament put an end to these pilgrimages in 1581, and Whithorn's importance dwindled, until it is now a quiet little town, much decayed, but still retaining a pride in the glories of its past.

St. Ninian's Country is called the Machars. It is a large triangle bounded by Luce Bay, Wigtown Bay and the road from Newton Stewart to Glenluce. Burrow Head is its apex. The peninsula is lowest on the eastern side, where a broad plain runs through Wigtown, Sorbie and Whithorn to the Isle of Whithorn, a rock-encircled harbour set with gaily coloured houses. On the western side the land is higher, and the Luce Bay shore more rugged. Port William is the only place of any size on this coast, although the holiday population of Monreith Bay must outstrip it in summer. The Machars is noted for large dairy farms which are nowadays conspicuous for their tall, green food storage tanks rather than for the red hay sheds, by which they were once so easily recognised. These farms produce the milk on which Wigtown's fame and prosperity are based—the manufacture of cheese and butter.

The little towns and villages in the Machars are gayer than those anywhere else in Scotland. Instead of grey granite or red sandstone, the houses are painted in bright colours—whitewash with red door and window-lintels, cream with blue lintels, and even pale green with turquoise. Everywhere you will see cottages being repaired and renovated for the Wigtown folk are suddenly realising that St. Ninian's Country could be a paradise for holidaymakers.

THE RHINNS

Behind Stranraer lies a low strip of land which links Loch Ryan and Luce Bay; were it not for this land the Rhinns of Galloway would be an island instead of a great coat-hook hanging on the end of Scotland and reaching as far south in latitude as Yorkshire.

The Rhinns is an area of contrasts—in the north it runs to the bleak point at the mouth of Loch Ryan where the winds sweep across the bare landscape without so much as a tree to stop them. In the south bold cliffs thrust themselves out towards England, Ireland and the Isle of Man, as if defying anyone to meddle with Scotland. Yet in between lies one of the most beautiful gardens in the whole of Scotland, a garden which is filled with plants and shrubs which one would scarcely expect to find outside the tropics.

The Rhinns shore of Loch Ryan has been much marred also, for a seaplane base was built opposite Cairnryan and abandoned in due course to decay under the moist, salt-laden winds that blow up the loch. Nevertheless, the village of Kirkcolm a few miles further on has not been spoilt; it still sits prettily above the loch.

On the North Channel lies the only place of any size in the Rhinns—Portpatrick, which had a splendid harbour and was the port from which the ferry service ran to Ireland a century ago. However, in 1874 Portpatrick was deserted for the more sheltered harbour of Stranraer, and Portpatrick died away to a quiet holiday resort set in a cove and flanked by towering cliffs.

Apart from Portpatrick all the villages are situated on the more sheltered Luce Bay side of the Rhinns, and the road from Stranraer passes through Stoneykirk and the holiday place of Sandhead, to Kirkmaiden, Drummore and the Mull of Galloway. About half way down the coast you must turn off to the right and cross the peninsula if you want to see the famous Logan Gardens, and the fishpond where the fish are so tame that they can be fed by hand. The pond was once the fresh fish larder of Logan House, but it is more than half a century since the last fish was netted for the pot. The fish are now only a tourist attraction, and they must be the best fed fish in the whole of Scotland.

South of Drummore the land begins to rise towards the Mull of Galloway, the 250-foot high cliffs at the foot of which they say nine tides meet. This is where Scotland begins and ends. From here you can see England, Ireland and the Isle of Man on a clear day, and at night the lighthouse, standing three hundred feet above the gurley water, winks out its warning to sailors that this is a wild shore and they should steer clear of it.

IV

BONNIE FECHTERS

WE know very little about the people who lived in South-west Scotland before the third century A.D., although there is evidence of them in a number of places. The main source of information about the earliest people is their tombs—large chambered stone-works built for communal burial, which are especially numerous in Galloway. The interiors of these tombs have been pillaged many centuries ago, and even the stonework has been carted away to build houses and castles, but here and there a few stones remain to indicate the presence of a grave.

The builders of these tombs probably came from Western Europe to settle first along the edge of the Firth of Clyde and later to move further afield. As relics of prehistoric inhabitants there are also standing stones dotted over the countryside, some of them decorated with primitive devices called cup and ring markings. These too, are most numerous in Galloway, and mostly lie within a short distance of the coast.

Later on the inhabitants built hill forts, the sites of which mean little to the untrained eye, but much to the archaeologist. These thick-walled forts were really townships in which communities lived together for safety from their enemies, and naturally they were built in a commanding position, usually a hilltop. Some-times, as at Traprain Law in East Lothian and Eildon Hill in Roxburghshire, they covered a wide area and must have housed a large number of people. Smaller forts are found on top of hills throughout Carrick and Galloway, again usually within a few miles of the coast.

In time the early occupants of Scotland progressed to build circular dwellings with immensely thick walls, which are known as brochs and, although the vast majority of known brochs are in the north of Scotland and the islands, there is one in Ayrshire at Camp Castle, near Kilmarnock, and there are others in the south of Wigtownshire. After brochs came duns, large fortified positions which housed a number of people, and crannogs, circular houses set on top of islands on the lochs. The islands were often artificial having been built up laboriously with boulders which were ferried out in small boats and dumped in the water. Duns extend throughout the South-west, and vestiges of crannogs have been discovered in many Galloway lochs.

All this adds up to little knowledge of the people of the South-west before the Romans arrived, and even the legions of the Emperor shed little civilising light on Scotland. In A.D. 80 Agricola led the Romans through Annandale and Lauderdale to the Forth and Clyde, and two years later the first forays were made into Dumfriesshire, Ayrshire and Galloway. The Romans found the country dour and inhospitable, with thick forest and marshland almost everywhere, and wild people who fought them fiercely living in crannogs on the lochs. Even in the forests there was no safety, for wolves, bears and wild boars roamed there. The Romans never subdued the tribes of the South-west—indeed, they could not hold Scotland and eventually had to withdraw behind Hadrian's Wall.

When the Romans finally left Britain about A.D. 400, the highly civilised southern half of the country was left open to attack from wild tribes in the north, and Danes, Angles, Jutes and Norsemen from Europe. All this resulted in several centuries of instability and the setting-up of a number of kingdoms, which united to form Scotland more or less as we know it today.

The main part of the country north of the Forth was Alban,

where the Picts lived. To the west the Scots arrived from Ireland to establish the kingdom of Dalriada in what is now Argyll. Strathclyde extended south from Loch Lomond through Renfrewshire, Ayrshire and Dumfriesshire into Cumberland and Westmorland. The Lothians formed part of Northumbria, and Galloway was a kingdom of its own. These kingdoms gradually came together until, in 1034, Duncan succeeded Malcolm II as ruler of Scotland.

Who were the people of Strathclyde and Galloway? Strathclyde was peopled with Brythonic-Britons who spoke a Celtic language which has become modern Welsh. Galloway was probably a Welsh kingdom, although its people, called Gallgaels, had Pictish and Scottish blood as well. Galloway was isolated from the rest of Scotland by hills and moors, and it remained apart from Scotland until well into the fourteenth century. Because of its isolation it also retained the Gaelic language until the eighteenth century.

Throughout history there have been injections of new blood into South-western Scotland—Angles from Northumbria, marauding Norsemen, Anglo-Normans in search of land, Irish colonising from across the North Channel, Highlanders displaced by war or famine, and in recent generations, a considerable number of Englishmen brought north by industry. At the time of the Plantation of Ulster in the seventeenth century, large numbers of Ayrshire and Galloway men settled in Ireland, and in the religious oppressions and wars which followed, some returned. In later times famine in Ireland forced thousand to cross to Scotland in search of work in the new industries which the industrial revolution brought, so that at the beginning of the nineteenth century it was said that there were constant streams of Irish beggars along the road from Portpatrick to Ayr, "some of whom", one commentator wrote, "like the debris of a moving glacier, would fall off by the way and get located in the district".

In the later nineteenth century too, bands of Highlanders and Irishmen came to this part of Scotland each year to gather the

harvest in and to plant and pick the potato crop. The invention of
the binder ended the need for itinerant harvest workers, but Irish
'tattie howkers' were still a regular feature of the farming scene
thirty years ago and, indeed, the version of the song, "Wha Saw
The Forty-Second", which we sang did not refer to the regiment
at all. It went:

> Wha saw the tattie howkers?
> Wha saw them gaun' awa'?
> Wha saw the tattie howkers,
> Sailing doon the Broomielaw?

Fewer Ayrshire farmers grow potatoes in quantity any more,
so the itinerant Irish potato pickers are seldom seen except on the
early potato farms along the coast. Over the years a large number
of these people must have remained behind when their countrymen returned home at the end of the season, and they have
leavened the stolid Ayrshire and Galloway Scot.

Within the South-west there has been movement of population,
and not simply of countrymen into the towns in search of work in
industry. Among the farming community of Galloway, one
commonly finds Ayrshire surnames (and temperaments too), for
many of them are descended from Ayrshire men whose skill built
up the fine dairying industry of Galloway in the latter part of the
nineteenth century. Farmers who moved south from Ayrshire
took their menservants and maids with them, so that whole
districts became thoroughly transformed into Ayrshire communities. In places, as many as half of the farming folk are descended from those incomers, and they retain much of the character
of their forefathers.

Through much of history one family has dominated all others
in South-west Scotland; indeed, the history of medieval Ayrshire
is largely their story. The Kennedys were well established in the
county by the thirteenth century, although their origins are said
to lie much further back in history, and one Caennad was the
father of King Cole, the prince of Strathclyde who gave his name

to Kyle in Ayrshire. At any rate most of the Kennedys who held
land in the South-west were descended from Sir Gilbert Kennedy
of Dunure, who lived during the second half of the fourteenth
century, and who probably traced his own ancestry to the Earls
of Carrick, a title which continues in the Royal family, with the
Prince of Wales as the present Earl. Sir Gilbert Kennedy's progeny
prospered and multiplied so that within a century there were
Kennedys from Ayr to the far south of Wigtownshire, and even
in the Stewartry of Kirkcudbright. The situation was summed up
in a rhyme:

> Twixt Wigtown and the toun of Ayr,
> Portpatrick and the Cruives of Cree,
> No man needs think for to bide there,
> Unless he court with Kennedie.

The Kennedys quickly established themselves in the Scottish
ascendancy; Gilbert's eldest son, James, married the daughter of
King Robert III, and one of their sons became the first Lord
Kennedy, while another was the famous Bishop Kennedy of St.
Andrews, who founded St. Salvators College there. In 1509, the
third Lord Kennedy was made Earl of Cassillis, and this heralded
a century during which the Kennedy sword ruled and took fearful
revenge on any who opposed or offended them.

When the second Earl of Cassillis quarrelled with Sir Hew
Loudon, Sheriff of Ayr, and was murdered by Loudon's men
among the sand dunes near Prestwick in 1537, the Kennedys swore
vengeance and marched north to sack the Campbell strongholds.
Later the Bargany Kennedys became embroiled in a quarrel
between the MacDowells of Garthland and the Gordons of
Lochinvar, and again blood flowed. However, the great Kennedy
quarrel involved Kennedy against Kennedy—Cassillis against
Bargany—and it included such revolting deeds as the roasting
alive of Allan Stewart, Commendator of Dunure, by Cassillis, and
the waylaying of Bargany on the road to Maybole. By 1601, when
the feud reached its climax, the Earl of Cassillis, abetted by his

uncle and former guardian, Sir Thomas Kennedy of Culzean, opposed Gilbert Kennedy of Bargany who was spurred on by his brother-in-law John Mure of Auchendrane, Walter Mure of Cloncaird, and his Kennedy kinsmen of Blairquhan, Bennan and Drummurchie.

For a brief moment towards the end of 1600 peace seemed likely when one of Culzean's daughters married Auchendrane's son, but a year later tempers were as hot as ever. In December 1601, Drummurchie and Bennan attempted to ambush Cassillis on his way to Maybole, and the Earl only escaped because he got word of the plot and took a different route. Cassillis' fury mounted when Bargany rode calmly past his house a week later on his way to Ayr. This was plain defiance, so Cassillis gathered together two hundred men, and waited for his enemy to return. On 11th December, Bargany set out to ride home through a snowstorm, accompanied by some eighty men, who included Mure of Auchendrane, Bennen and Drummurchie. Near Brockloch on the moors above Maybole they encountered Cassillis' men and tried to bypass them, but the Cassillis party would not let them ride on. While most of his party held back Bargany led four of his men into the enemy ranks. The Galloway novelist S. R. Crockett captured this climax of the Kennedy feud in his novel *The Grey Man*—"There were three that he held at arm's length," wrote Crockett, "all the while crying out for the Earl, and trying fiercely to break through the spearmen, who stood like a fence about the person of Cassillis. 'Where is my lord himself?' he cried. 'Let him now keep promise, come out like a man to break a tree with me.' So went the fight of one against many, and such deeds of valiance saw I never any man do in this realm of Scotland."

Then Cassillis horsemen attacked, and Bargany was wounded. He was carried to Maybole and later to Ayr, where he died five days later.

Cassillis managed to convince the powers in Edinburgh that he had not set out to murder Bargany, but merely to arrest Drummurchie, and this was believed. The final tragic act in the feud was the murder of Culzean by Bennan and Drummurchie, but it was dearly bought revenge, for they were outlawed. Within a generation the lands of Bargany had to be sold, and Cassillis was left supreme.

Religious and economic upheavals of the seventeenth century completed the work of destroying the Kennedys, as many branches of the family were forced to sell off their lands to pay fines or debts. By the end of the century, destruction was absolute —except for the Cassillis branch, which was given the title Marquis of Ailsa in 1830. Culzean was the seat of the Ailsas until after the Second World War, when it was handed over to the National Trust for Scotland and opened to the public. For a time the Ailsas continued to live in a wing of the castle, but some years ago they moved back to Cassillis, the original home of that branch of the family, that fine old fortress from which their ancestors carried on so much of the feuding which set the family on the path to fortune.

As the Kennedy star waned in Carrick in the seventeenth century, Cathcarts, Hunter-Blairs, and others came in. Further disruption followed the collapse of the Ayr Bank in the later eighteenth century when many old families were ruined and much of the land of Ayrshire was put on the market. New rich now began to come in, followed by the merchant princes who made fortunes in the Industrial Revolution. This process was accelerated during the nineteenth century when families like Coats, the Paisley thread firm bought Auchendrane, and James Baird, the iron and coal master, built Cambusdoon House. The older families were none too happy about the change, and it is said that when Baird began to build Cambusdoon some of the Cathcarts wrote in fear that he might be turning the place into some great factory. Baird's reply was brief and businesslike. "When there is a lum needed," he wrote, "there'll be a lum biggit."

In Kyle the Craufurds and Campbells were powerful, with branches dispersed throughout the district. The Craufurds were the most numerous family in Kyle although, according to Paterson who wrote the history of the county, the Reids ran them a close second, about the time of the Reformation. Other fine Scottish names were also well represented—the Wallaces in Sundrum, Dreghorn, Craigie and Auchincruive, Blairs in Adamton, Cathcarts in Carbieston, and Bailies in Monkton until they were ruined in the South Sea Bubble fiasco. To the north were Fullartons of Fullarton, and families of Cunningham district overflowed into Kyle—the Montgomeries and the Boyds among them. Perhaps the best-known name in Kyle is Boswell of Auchinleck, a family which originated in Fife and only came to Ayrshire in 1504. This was the family that bred James Boswell, Dr. Johnson's companion and biographer.

But even the greatest houses must go into eclipse, and the end of the Kyle families was summed-up in one of those rhymes of which people in our district seem so fond:

> Sundrum shall sink,
> Auchincruive shall fa',
> And the name of Cathcart
> Shall in time wear awa'.

Sundrum is now a hotel; Auchincruive houses the West of Scotland Agricultural College; and the Cathcarts are no longer great landowners in the county.

In upper Nithsdale the principal families were the Crichtons of Sanquhar, who were said to have come from Hungary, and the Douglases of Drumlanrig—both of which families have now vanished into the Scottish peerage, the Crichtons as Marquises of Bute and the Douglases as Dukes of Buccleuch. Further down Nithsdale lived the Maxwells who stood as a buffer between England and Scotland in the difficult centuries of raid and counter raid. The centre of Maxwell power was Caerlaverock Castle, just south of Dumfries, but they married into the other Dumfriesshire families—the Carlyles, Murrays, Johnstones and Herries, the last of whom were the ultimate Maxwell heirs. The Maxwells became the Earls of Nithsdale and their power is recalled in the name of Maxwelltown, where this powerful family annexed Lincluden Abbey after the Reformation for its own mansion. At Moniaive, too, is Maxwelton House where Annie Laurie was born to inspire Scotland's most famous love song of all time. William Douglas of Fingland wooed her with the verse:

> She's backit like the peacock,
> She's breistit like the swan,
> She's jimp about the middle,
> Her waist ye weel may span;
> Her waist ye weel may span,
> And she has a rolling eye,
> And for Bonnie Annie Laurie
> I'd lay me doon and die.

Annie Laurie was not won with that verse, for she upped and married Fergusson of Craigdarroch, a little to the north of Maxwelton House. It was Lady John Scott, the nineteenth-century poetess, who turned Douglas's poem into something more likely to win a wife:

> Maxwelton braes are bonnie
> Where early fa's the dew.
> It was there that Annie Laurie
> Gied me her promise true.
> Gied me her promise true,
> That ne'er forgot shall be.
> And for Bonnie Annie Laurie
> I would lay me doon and dee.

The first Lord of Galloway of whom we know, is Fergus, a devout man, who built a monastery in the province. His sons, Roland and Uchtred became joint Lords of Galloway and eventually split the province into Galloway and Carrick. The Carrick descendants flourished as Kennedys to rule much of Wigtownshire as well, but when they declined their place was taken by the Dalrymples of Stair, a family who 'made money as lawyers and

well understood the principle of securities in land'. It is ironic that
the Dalrymples should have ousted the Kennedys, for the Stair
surname was derived from the barony of Dalrymple in Ayrshire,
and the Kennedys had usurped that some centuries earlier. As
Earls of Stair the Dalrymples still flourish at Castle Kennedy.

Throughout Wigtownshire there has always been a fair inter-
change with families from Ayrshire, the Borders and Ireland—
Campbells, Douglases and Cathcarts among them. However, the
MacDowalls of Garthland and their branches were the chief
family of the Rhinns, while McCullochs and Stewarts were numerous in the Machars and on the Kirkcudbright borders. The
Stewarts of Garlies became the Earls of Galloway.

In the Stewartry one encounters 'Macs' in many shapes and
forms—McNeys, M'Taggarts, McCombs and so on, although
they have a disconcerting habit of dropping the 'Mac' and referr-
ing to themselves as Ney, Taggart and Comb. They have even
been known to take a perfectly reasonable name and add a 'Mac'
to it—much to the confusion of the owner of the name. However,
the great names hereabout are the Gordons of Lochinvar and the
Maclellans of Kirkcudbright. These families were as wild as the
Kennedys, and one can well imagine young Lochinvar of Sir
Walter Scott's *Marmion* coming out of the West, armed only with
his broadsword, to snatch away a bride from under the nose of
the 'laggard in love', to whom she was to be married.

> There was racing and chasing in Canonbie Lee,
> But the lost bride of Netherby ne'er did they see.
> So daring in love, and so dauntless in war,
> Have ye e'er heard of gallant like young Lochinvar?

Many young Lochinvars rode out of the West to cause trouble.
On 11th July 1526, James Gordon of Lochinvar and Sir William
Douglas of Drumlanrig and their followers murdered Thomas
Maclellan of Bombie in the High Street of Edinburgh. In 1600
another Gordon fell out with the Bargany Kennedys over which
of them should be Admiral on the South-west coast. This Gordon

seems to have surpassed all others at making trouble, for he was accused of murder twice, he rescued a prisoner in Edinburgh's High Street, and even his own mother had to seek protection against his violence. It was his son who became the first Viscount Kenmure in 1633, but the Gordons could not stay out of trouble for long—the sixth Viscount joined the Old Pretender in the 1715 Rebellion, and was captured at Preston.

The Maclellans, who were closely associated with the town of Kirkcudbright, feuded with the Gordons, and there was little to choose between the two factions. As a young man the son of the Maclellan murdered by Lochinvar and Drumlanrig in the High Street of Edinburgh, was wild and constantly in trouble with authority, but he sobered down later and was created Lord Kirkcudbright.

Times have changed, and feuding is over in the South-west; many of these ancient families have vanished and their surnames remain only as names of parishes, villages or streets. Perhaps this is as well, for the rule of the sword did no good. It turned what might have been a golden day of peace, tolerance and progress into a night of medieval turmoil, which lasted right into the seventeenth century. One can only speculate on what the present might have been, were it not for that troubled sixteenth century when feuding was at its height. Certainly it would have made the people very different, for the South-western Scot is what he is because of the past.

Farm cat at Ellisland
Clatteringshaws Dam, part of Galloway power scheme

SAINTS AND SINNERS

"If there be holy ground anywhere in Scotland which will not yield even to Iona in venerable antiquity, it is this grey corner of our country where, about the year 400 after Christ, St. Ninian preached the Gospel to our Celtic forefathers," wrote the nineteenth-century Scottish Professor John Stuart Blackie when he visited Whithorn.

We know very little of Ninian or of his work, for the first writings about him which we have are those of Bede who lived three centuries later. Nevertheless, archaeologists have uncovered facts which indicate that these first writings, although based on tradition, contain much truth.

The mixture of legend and fact which we have about Ninian indicates that he was the son of a British prince, that he studied in Rome, and that he returned to his native country to spread Christianity both among his own people as widely as the land of the Southern Picts—which means as far away as the Grampians—long before Columba came to Iona. Ninian built a stone church at Whithorn, and stone buildings were so unusual in those days that the church was given the Latin name of Candida Casa, the White House. Ninian's church was named after St. Martin of Tours, probably because he had stopped there for a time on his way home from Rome. Although every vestige of Ninian's church above ground has vanished, archaeologists have proved conclusively that

Caravans line the disused railway at Maidens
Sermon on the rocks below Girvan

it stood on the site of the ruined Priory just behind the main street of Whithorn.

As an example of tradition proving well founded, there is a cave a few miles from Whithorn, on the Luce Bay shore at the foot of Physgill Glen, which has long been linked with Ninian, although for centuries there was no proof of any such association. Then, in the 'seventies of the last century, a cross was found carved on the rock just to the inside of the cave. That was the beginning—other crosses dating from very early times were found, proving that this was, indeed, the cave to which Ninian retired to meditate and pray.

Just beside the entrance to the Priory churchyard stands a cottage which has been turned into a museum to hold many of the relics from the cave, and other precious pieces of stone which have been found around Whithorn. These are our only tangible link with the first Christians of Scotland, and often no more than a fragment of a stone cross has survived. Occasionally however, a whole stone remains, as in the case of the *Latinus Stone*, a slender, rough pillar bearing the inscription in Latin: "We praise the Lord. Latinus, aged 35, and his daughter, aged 4 (lie) here. This monument was erected by grandson Barrovadus." This is the earliest Christian memorial in Scotland, for it dates from about A.D. 450, almost all the way back to Ninian himself. The wording of the inscriptions and the type of lettering used help to identify and date these stones; for example, a cross found along the Isle of Whithorn road just outside Whithorn, has been identified as belonging to the seventh century, simply because the lettering of the inscription is of a type which ceased to be used after that time. The wording on this stone, "The place of Peter The Apostle", indicates that it marked a small oratory dedicated to St. Peter close to the original monastery.

Wigtownshire is rich in these early Christian monuments, and others which span the years from the fifth to the twelfth centuries have been found at Kirkmadrine, in the Rhinns. The oldest stones at Kirkmadrine are two rough pillars with crosses which were used as gateposts for many years. The first bears a cross and the Chi-Rho symbol (the first two letters of the Greek word *Christos*), and the wording "Here lie the holy and chief priests, Ides, Viventius and Mavorius". Unfortunately only a tiny part of the inscription on the second pillar remains: " . . .s and Florentius". Presumably, it was a similar memorial to other priests.

St. Ninian's monastery became a far-famed seat of learning as well as a centre from which missionaries went out to convert men to Christianity, and even after the Northumbrians conquered Galloway, the monastery continued to exist. Indeed, the first break came only when the Vikings invaded and conquered in the eleventh century. In the following century, when Fergus became Lord of Galloway, Whithorn had its bishopric restored, and from then until the Reformation four hundred years later it was the greatest place of pilgrimage in the whole of Scotland. For centuries Scottish kings came to the shrine of St. Ninian to cure their ills, to ask his help or simply to seek his blessing—Robert the Bruce came in a last attempt to cure his leprosy shortly before his death, his son David II to remove arrowheads which were lodged in his body in battle, and the Stewarts in almost constant succession from James I to Queen Mary. Not all the royal pilgrims made a saintly progress to Ninian's tomb. James IV, for example, is said to have become enamoured of Lord Kennedy's daughter Janet when he met her on his way to Whithorn about 1499, and she bore him a son who became James, Earl of Moray. To commemorate these royal progresses the archway which leads from George Street to Whithorn Priory has the royal arms of Scotland set above it, and it is decorated with a painting of Queen Mary on a pilgrimage to Whithorn.

Many pilgrims arrived by sea at the Isle of Whithorn, where a little ruined chapel stands close to the harbour. Although it has been said to be Ninian's chapel, this was probably built much later for the benefit of arriving and departing pilgrims.

The Reformation brought these pilgrimages to an end, and thereafter Whithorn declined. Visitors who come to Ninian's shrine today, mostly arrive by motor-car in twos and threes, for there are no great processions as in the Middle Ages. There is no longer need for anyone to petition (as Margaret, Countess of Douglas did in 1441) for an indulgence to help to rebuild the bridge over the Bladnoch because it was the place where Whithorn pilgrims assembled.

From Whithorn Christianity spread far into Scotland, and, although one associates the great abbeys with the Border counties of Roxburgh and Selkirk, the South-west is every bit as rich in them. The rise of these religious houses began in the twelfth century when Fergus, the first Lord of Galloway, and David I, sixth son of saintly Queen Margaret of Scotland, founded several abbeys, of which only gaunt stones remain. Even in decay the abbeys are exquisite, and it is easy to imagine them in their glory five hundred years ago. Although pillaged for secular building over the centuries following the Reformation, most of the abbeys are now in the custody of the Ministry of Public Buildings and Works, and the stonework has been preserved and grounds set out as lawns.

The first of the abbeys of the South-west was Dundrennan, which stands among the neat folds of the Kirkcudbright country-side. Dundrennan dates from 1142, and like its contemporary Melrose, it was colonised by the Cistercians of Rievaulx in Yorkshire. Dundrennan is one of the finest of the Scottish abbeys, with its great west doorway testifying to the glory of its noblest days. In ruin it has a sadness that is fitting for the place where Mary Queen of Scots spent her last night in Scotland.

Eighteen years later, in 1160, Fergus founded Saulseat, close by the present-day town of Stranraer. Saulseat never was rich, but its lands were attractive enough to be coveted and seized by power-hungry Kennedys at the Reformation, who used the stones of Saulseat for building, principally for Castle Kennedy. As a result the abbey has vanished from the face of Scotland, and even its name is forgotten today.

Fergus's sons, Uchtred and Roland, founded religious houses too. First Uchtred established Lincluden across the Nith from

Dumfries, in what is now Maxwelltown. For the first two hundred and fifty years of its existence Lincluden was occupied by Benedictine nuns until they were expelled in the fourteenth century by Archibald Douglas, who erected a college with provost and canons, which remained at Lincluden until the Reformation when Lincluden was turned into a house for the Maxwell family. Little remains of Lincluden, save the chancel of the little fifteenth-century church which was built by William Douglas, Duke of Touraine and his wife, Princess Margaret of Scotland. Douglas was one of those Scots who fought against the English in France and although he lies in the cathedral of Tours, his wife's tomb is at Lincluden. Fergus's other son, Roland, founded Glenluce in the last decade of the twelfth century, and at the Reformation this abbey also went to the Kennedys. Cassillis was negotiating for the lease of the abbey lands when the abbot was inconsiderate enough to die, so he persuaded one of the monks to forge the abbot's signature and then arranged for the monk to be murdered. In turn the monk's murderer was accused of theft by another Kennedy and hanged—"And sa the landis of Glenluce was conqueist." Little is now left of the abbey buildings, although the chapter house and water system are intact enough to tell much about the way in which the monks lived.

After the foundation of Glenluce came Crossraguel in Carrick, a Cluniac abbey connected with Paisley, established by Duncan, Earl of Carrick in 1214. Crossraguel is in the heart of the Kennedy country, so it is not surprising that the Kennedys held sway there during its existence as a religious house, and that they took it over after the Reformation. Crossraguel may not be as impressive as the great Border abbeys, but it is surprisingly well preserved so that one can still see the church, cloisters, sacristry, chapter house, refectory, and even the abbot's house and dovecot much as they were before the Reformation. Today Crossraguel is one of the most beautiful tourists sights of Ayrshire—marred only by the most evil-smelling public lavatory in the county, which is appropriately located in the dungeons.

The last of the great abbeys of the South-west is Sweetheart, the beautiful abbey which Devorgilla established near Dumfries in 1273. Even in ruin Sweetheart stands red and majestic behind the red village of New Abbey. It is a glorious memorial to true love, for Devorgilla was buried there, with her husband's heart laid on her breast. Devorgilla and Balliol have other memorials—Balliol College in Oxford, the old bridge across the Nith at Dumfries, monasteries at Wigtown and Dumfries—but their real memorial in Scotland is the glowing abbey of *Dulce Cora*.

Just as Devorgilla's monasteries in Wigtown and Dumfries have vanished without trace, so have the monasteries of the Black Friars and the Grey Friars in Ayr, which the zealous reforming burgesses of Ayr pulled down. And even the ancient church of St. John the Baptist in Ayr only escaped at the Reformation to be turned into an armoury by Cromwell a century later. Maybole's Collegiate Church, which dates from 1373, also survived, and it stands today on a peaceful, well-kept triangle of land close to the centre of the town. The street that leads from the High Street to the church is now called John Knox Street—and that brings us to Protestantism with a vengeance.

Walking down John Knox Street—so steep a hill that the neat, new houses stand in stepped rows—one could hardly guess that this is where one of the 'battles' of the Reformation took place. Abbot Quintin Kennedy of Crossraguel issued a challenge from the pulpit of Kirkoswald church to any of the reformers to debate the new religion, and John Knox hastened to accept. However, the abbot cannily stayed at home and Knox had the pulpit to himself. Knox persisted, and the debate took place in the house of the Provost of Maybole Collegiate Church, before eighty people who packed themselves into the little house. For three days the two argued, but neither would give way, and each claimed victory in the end. Whatever the outcome of the Maybole debate Knox won the final victory in Scotland, and Presbyterianism was established as the national religion—a brand of Presbyterianism that was tempered as finely as high quality steel by the opposition and oppression which it met in the century after its establishment.

Knox's victory was consolidated by his son-in-law, John Welsh, who was minister at Ayr for five years. Welsh was born at Dunscore in Dumfriesshire in 1570, and he entered the ministry at Kirkcudbright, but soon found himself outlawed for daring to speak against James VI. By 1600 he had been forgiven, and moved to Ayr, where he played an important part in ending the feuds between the Kennedys and their enemies. It was said that Welsh used to rush between the fighting men, unarmed, to separate them, and that he then placed a table in the street and made the opposing factions sit down at it and settle their quarrel. Ayr people were grateful to Welsh, and he enjoyed tremendous popularity among them. When he was thrown into Blackness Castle for taking part in an unlawful General Assembly of the Kirk at Aberdeen, the Town Council voted £10 "to the minister's wyf to pay her expenses in ganging to her husband".

Poor Welsh was banished, and for sixteen years he wandered on the Continent, spreading Protestantism. At length his health began to fail and he longed to see home again, so he came to London in 1622 to petition James VI for leave to return to Scotland. His wife was permitted to plead for her husband:

"Who was your father?" asked the King.

"John Knox," she replied.

"Knox and Welsh," cried James. "The Devil never made sic a match as that."

John Knox's daughter had an answer: "It's right like, sir, for we never speired his advice."

James offered to repeal the sentence of banishment if Welsh would accept bishops, but even though he longed for home Welsh would not agree, and he died in London the same year.

If the generations of Knox and Welsh laid the foundations of Presbyterianism, it took another century to consolidate their work —a bitter hundred years in which all South-west Scotland was a battlefield, and every man, woman and child a soldier of the Kirk. This was the era of the Covenanters; the generation of oppression which culminated in the Killing Time of 1684-5, and it sharpened the edge of Presbyterianism and moulded the character of the people perhaps more than any other factor in their history.

The Covenanters were those who pledged themselves by the National Covenant of 1638, and the Solemn League and Covenant of 1640 to resist the imposition of episcopacy and all that goes with it in their country. The worst of the troubles began twenty years later when Charles II, safely restored to the throne, began to impose the policies of his father and grandfather, and ministers appointed since 1649 were ordered to be re-ordained by bishops or to leave their parishes. About 270 chose expulsion—by far the great majority of them in the South-west. In Ayrshire alone, two in every three ministers were turned out of their living.

Despite heavy fines, threats of imprisonment, banishment to the plantations and even death, the people refused to attend churches where the pulpits were filled by puppets appointed by the king, and instead they gathered in great open-air meetings called conventicles to hear their own ministers preach. Government troops scoured the countryside arresting and murdering, and a rabble of Highlanders billeted on the area earned the title *The Highland Host*, as they plundered the countryside. The persecution culminated in the Killing Time of 1684-5, when terrible vengeance was wrought on the Covenanters, and worn gravestones and carefully-tended monuments stand everywhere in the South-west to remind us of the cost of preserving our religious freedom.

In the century following a stonemason, Robert Paterson—Old Mortality of Sir Walter Scott's novels, travelled the Galloway countryside on his white pony tending and restoring these monuments. Although Paterson belonged to Balmaclellan and a stone in the churchyard there records this work which Paterson took upon himself voluntarily, he actually lies in the kirkyard at Caerlaverock, where he died as a result of a fall from his pony. There are several sculptures depicting Old Mortality and his work—one in the grounds of the Holme House at Balmaclellan, another in Dumfries and one at Laurel Hill Cemetery in Philadelphia.

The sculptor responsible for these works was John Corrie, who was born at Lochfoot in Dumfriesshire, but by chance he too is linked with Balmaclellan. His descendant Alexander Corrie is proprietor of a garage and agricultural implement works in the village, and beside the petrol pumps stand two fine stone figures, one of a Cameronian and the other of Old Mortality at work.

Although the skirmish at Drumclog was the only battle that took place in the South-west during the campaign against the Covenanters, the fight was carried on among the hills of Ayrshire and Galloway. Conventicles were held throughout the country, but the greatest in the South-west was the one at Craigdow Hill near Maybole, in August 1678, when seven thousand people listened for two days to the preaching of men like John Welsh, the great grandson of John Knox, and Richard Cameron, who later met a Covenanter's death at Aird's Moss in the high back country of Ayrshire. Cameron and his men had renounced King Charles by a declaration made at Sanquhar in 1680, and for a month they were hunted among the hills until they were betrayed and cornered at Aird's Moss. "Lord, spare the green, and take the ripe," said Cameron, as he and his men began to fight for their lives. Cameron and eight of his men died there on the moor; others were taken to Edinburgh and executed.

There was a touch of grim humour in the men who led the conventicles. At Drumclog Thomas Douglas was preaching when the alarm went up that Claverhouse was approaching. Douglas ended the service with the exhortation, "Ye have got the theory; now for the practice", and the armed men came to the front to shield the elderly and the women from the soldiers.

Stories of the Covenanters in the South-west are legion, and that of John Brown of Priesthill is typical enough. Brown was cutting peats one day near his home, which lay in the hills above Muirkirk, when Claverhouse came on him and ordered him to take oaths abjuring the Covenants and swearing never to rise against the king. He refused, and was shot down in front of his wife and children. "What think you of your goodman now?"

Graham asked Brown's wife, as she knelt over her dead husband. "I aye thocht muckle o' him, and I think mair o' him now than ever," she replied.

In Galloway, too, stories of suffering were numerous. In February 1685, Captain Bruce and his Dragoons who had been scouring the Galloway hills, came on a party of Covenanters at Lochenkit, near Kirkpatrick Durham. Four of them, John Gordon, William Stewart, John Wallace and William Heron were shot, and two others, Edward Gordon and Alexander M'Cubbin were taken to Irongray church where they were hanged from a tree. The King's men were zealous in their routing-out of Covenanters —Colonel James Douglas, who shot Robert McWhae at his home at Kirkandrews, also murdered the Glen Trool martyrs—James and Robert Duns, Thomas and John Stevensons, James McClure, and Andrew McCall, as they prayed at Caldons, near the present-day camping site at Loch Trool.

The most appalling crime of the Killing Time was the barbaric execution of an elderly woman and a girl at Wigtown in 1685. Margaret MacLauchlan was over sixty, but Margaret Wilson was only eighteen when the two were tried and sentenced to be tied to stakes on the Solway Sands and left to drown as the tide came in. Crowds gathered on the shore to see the sentence carried out, and a century afterwards there was still a feeling of shock as old people told how their grandfathers had described the terrible crime. As so often happens, cruelty failed to break the spirit of the oppressed; the two graves in Wigtown Churchyard served instead to steel the Covenanters to the fight, and to give them determination to win.

Appropriately, a memorial to "the noble army of martyrs in Galloway and other parts of Scotland", stands on Windy Hill, the highest point around Wigtown, to remind us of these men and women of whom Macaulay wrote: "They were easily defeated, and mercilessly punished, but neither defeat nor punishment could subdue their spirit. Hunted down like wild beasts, tortured till their bones were beaten flat, imprisoned by hundreds, hanged by scores, exposed at one time to the mercy of troops of marauders from the Highlands, they still stood at bay in a mood so savage that the boldest and mightiest oppressor could not but dread the audacity of their despair."

These were the Covenanters; their descendants have inherited much of their character.

Presbyterians have earned the reputation of being fighting folk —and for proof the story of almost every congregation in the last two centuries is littered with schisms and secessions.

Put two Presbyterians together and the chances are that within a month fifty per cent of them will be on the Communion Roll of the Auld or Established Kirk, and fifty per cent will have seceded.

Even within the societies which are part of the communal life, there are frequent quarrels and walk-outs which result in bitter and long-lasting feuds. It would be wrong to say that Presbyterians are the only people who indulge in such ongoings, but they are certainly highly skilled in the art of feuding.

It is not really surprising that the South-western Scot holds his opinions—especially his religious ones—strongly enough to fall out with anyone who opposes them. After all he was prepared to die for them during Covenanting times, so he had to be sure they were worth dying for.

The agricultural revolution of the latter part of the eighteenth century brought such social upheaval to the South-west that the old way of life vanished and many country folk were forced into the towns. The resulting insecurity led to profligacy, sexual licence and excessive drinking. New religious cults flourished, some of them anti-Christian, and others just odd. The best remembered of these strange sects was the Buchanites, the followers of Mrs. Buchan, a Banffshire innkeeper's daughter who flattered the Irvine minister, the Rev. Hugh Whyte, so successfully that he invited her to come to the town where she set up her sect. 'Luckie' Buchan talked of a new Coming of the Messiah, and of the translation to Heaven of herself and her followers at an appointed time. Irvine folk stood her nonsense for a time, but the Buchanites were eventually driven out to seek their new Jerusalem elsewhere. In the crowd which watched the departure of the sect was a small boy with a keen eye—the future novelist John Galt. Galt later recalled the departure of the psalm singing band of men and women headed by Mrs. Buchan as they set out for Closeburn in Dumfriesshire where they settled to await their elevation to Heaven. Mrs. Buchan and her followers spent the time at Closeburn singing hymns and praying until the appointed arrived. Joseph Train described the elevation:

On a particular height three platforms were erected, as if so many springboards, for the more distinguished of the body, the centre one being several feet higher than the others, and allotted to the special use of Mrs. Buchan, so that she might gain a somewhat earlier ascent, leading the way, and the flock following in promiscuous order. The whole fraternity, in full expectation of immediate ascent, had had their heads closely shaved, with the exception of a little tuft at the top by which the angels might grasp them and waft them to glory. All were in readiness by an early hour, the platforms were occupied, and the sound of hymn-singing in all its ecstacy rose and floated far away among the hills. A slight breeze sprang up, and this was construed as heralding the angelic approach, the cause being the action of celestial wings through the air. All at once a sudden blast swept over the scene, the platforms, with their occupants, were violently overturned, and an ignominious fall put an end to the ascension.

Not surprisingly Mrs. Buchan was no longer a power in the land, although she did keep a few followers until her death in 1791. The last of the Buchanites died in 1848.

The eighteenth century was a time of much dissent within the Kirk on the question of whether ministers should be appointed by patrons or by the congregations, and although this really only came to a head with the Disruption in the following century, it was an important issue in Burns's lifetime. In 1763 when William Lindsay was appointed Minister of Kilmarnock by Lord Glencairn, the Congregation showed their opposition by pelting him with offensive missiles. Nonetheless, the patron had his way and Lindsay stayed.

In his *Annals of the Parish* John Galt caught the spirit of the people who had a minister foisted on them and the feelings of the luckless minister also. This was the new minister's arrival at Dreghorn:

It was a great affair; for I was put in by the patron, and the people knew nothing whatsoever of me, and their hearts were stirred into strife on the occasion, and they did all that lay within the compass of their power to keep me out, insomuch that there was obliged to be a guard of soldiers to protect the presbytery; and it was a thing that made my heart grieve when I heard the drum beating and the fife playing as we were going to the kirk. The people were really mad and vicious, and flung dirt upon us as we passed, and reviled us all, and held out the finger of scorn at me; but I endured it with a resigned spirit, compassionating their wilfulness and blindness. Poor old Mr. Kilfuddy of the Brachill got such a clash of glar on the side of the face, that his eye was almost extinguished.

When we got to the kirk door, it was found to be nailed up, so as by no possibility to be opened. The sergeant of the soldiers wanted to break it, but I was afraid that the heritors would grudge and complain of the expense of a new door, and I supplicated him to let it be as it was; we were therefore obligated to go in by a window, and the crowd followed us in the most unreverent manner, making the Lord's house like an inn on a fair-day with their grievous yelly-hooing. During the time of the psalm and the sermon they behaved themselves better, but when the induction came on the clamour was dreadful; and Thomas Thorl, the weaver, a pious zealot, in that time, got up and protested, and said: "Verily, verily, I say unto you, he that entereth not by the door into the sheepfold; but climbeth up some other way, the same is a thief and a robber". And I thought I would have a hard and sore time of it with such an outstrapolous people. Mr. Given, that was then the minister of Lugton, was a jocose man, and would have his joke even at a solemnity. When the laying of the hands upon me was a-doing, he could not get near enough to put on his, but he stretched out his staff and touched my head, and said, to the great diversion of the rest: "This will do well enough—timber to timber"; but it was an unfriendly saying of Mr. Given, considering the time and the place, and the temper of my people.

After the ceremony we then got out at the window, and it was a heavy day to me; but we went to the manse, and there we had an excellent dinner, which Mrs. Watts of the new inn of Irville prepared at my request, and sent her chaise-driver to serve, for he was likewise her waiter, she having then but one chaise, and that not often called for.

However, the folk were good enough at heart and the following day the minister's worst enemy greeted him kindly enough at his house: "Come in, sir, and ease yourself; this will never do: the clergy are God's corbies, and for their Master's sake it behoves us to respect them. There was no ane in the whole parish mair against you than myself, but this early visitation is a symptom of grace that I couldna have expectit from a bird out of the nest of patronage."

The great issue of Burns's time, however, was Calvinism against a more enlightened form of Presbyterianism—Auld Lichts versus New Lichts—and Burns's pen contributed to this quarrel, at the same time immortalizing many Ayrshire ministers of the day.

Today we tend to take Burns's side in this quarrel, and we see the schism against the background of present-day Ayrshire rather than against the eighteenth century when the people as a whole were somewhat uneducated and the discipline imposed by the Kirk was exerted to preserve some measure of decency and respectability. By all means let us join Burns in mocking the hypocrites, but let us also remember the poet's own lewdness by standards of the eighteenth century or any other age.

Many ministers are remembered because of Burns. In Ayr there were Dr. McGill, leader of the Moderates, and his arch enemy William Peebles of Newton-on-Ayr whose poetry Burns scorned as much as his religious views. When Peebles used paradox (rather cleverly, I think) and wrote "bound in liberty's endearing chain", Burns retaliated:

Poet Willie! Poet Willie!
Gie the doctor a volley
Wi' your "Liberty's Chain" and your wit.

The ministers of Burns's day ranged from William Dalrymple
of Ayr Auld Kirk—'D'rymple mild' of "The Kirk's Alarm" who
baptised the poet—to Dr. William Auld of Mauchline, who is best
remembered, rather undeservedly, as the butt of Burns's satire.
'Daddy' Auld was as narrow and unyielding as any of his ilk in
eighteenth-century Ayrshire, and he richly deserved the scourging
he received for his attacks on Gavin Hamilton. At the same time
he was a sincere man deeply interested in his congregation, most
of whom were attached to him, too. And he did have a problem
parishioner in the erring Robert Burns.

In Kilmarnock there were the Auld Lichts James Oliphant of
the High Kirk and James Mackinlay of the Laigh Kirk who both
received glancing blows from the poet's pen, and even Moderates
like Mackinlay's predecessors at the Laigh Kirk, John Robertson
and John Mutrie did not escape. Of them he wrote:

Mutrie and you were just a match,
We never had sic two drones;
Auld Hornie did the Laigh Kirk watch,
Just like the winkin' baudrons.

Another Kilmarnock minister, John Russell, who scourged his
congregation like a black frost among the May blossom, quarrelled with Alexander Moodie of Riccarton and gave Burns
inspiration for his satire "The Twa Herds".

The Disruption of 1843 split the Church of Scotland in the
South-west every bit as badly as elsewhere, and there were many
ministers from Ayrshire and Galloway among the 451 who walked
out of the Established Kirk on that day in May to form the Free
Church. Once again ministers were prepared to suffer for their
beliefs, and many of them did suffer very real hardship. Burns's
nephew, the Rev. Thomas Burns of Monkton, spent many lean
years building a Free Kirk congregation in Prestwick—often on the

verge of starvation—before he left for New Zealand as one of the leaders of the party which founded Dunedin.

Until reunion in 1929 there were opposing churches in many a small parish which could ill afford the waste of duplication and dissent—many small towns had three churches. However, the farming folk largely stood by the Established Kirk, and looked on any other denomination or brand of Presbyterianism with suspicion. It is hard for outsiders to realise how complete the Established Kirk's domination was in places—in my own village, Minishant, during the 1930s the entire community was Auld Kirk, apart from a spell when there was one Roman Catholic family in the village. Indeed, when the Rev. David Swan came visiting he automatically called on the Roman Catholics as well, with no idea of proselytising, but I suspect just because he was in the habit of calling at every house wherever he went.

The Church of Scotland remains dominant in the South-west, although the Third Statistical Account revealed that there are close on thirty brands of religion in Ayrshire alone—among them the Church of Christ's single congregation in the Doon Valley mining village of Pennyvenie, and the Elim Four Square Gospellers in Ayr. Oddly enough there is only one congregation of Reformed Presbyterians—the Cameronians of Covenanting times —left and that is situated at Stranraer. In Ayrshire there is only one Methodist Church, one Friends' Meeting House, and one Jewish Synagogue. Even the Episcopal Church is weak, and what strength it has it derives from the aristocracy (who are educated almost exclusively in England), and from Englishmen who have come to Scotland to work. The influx of workers from south of the Border counterbalances the decline of the landed gentry, but the Episcopal Church continues to be referred to by the local people as the 'English Kirk'—a term which explains its form of service and their feeling towards it.

The Roman Catholic Church, too, is a comparatively unimportant influence in the South-west. At the Reformation most South-westerners turned, and the Catholicism has only returned

Loch Trool, cradle of Scotland's nationhood
Bruce's Stone, Loch Trool
Poosie Nansie's Inn, Mauchline

within the last century with the influx of Irish immigrants. Naturally it is strongest in the industrial areas, and in the western part of Wigtownshire, which lies closest to Ireland. However, Catholicism accounts for only about eight per cent of the population, and there are still parishes which do not have a single Roman Catholic in them.

The Church of Scotland therefore remains dominant, not only numerically, but in the whole life of the community. It is not afraid to pronounce on the moral issues, as the report of any Presbytery meeting will show. Indeed, the Presbytery meeting often gains more column inches in the local press than that of the town or county council.

It maintains its position despite the drift of people from the country areas into towns or even south to the industrial cities of England. Although this and the social upheavals resulting from two World Wars have influenced the pattern of living greatly, there has been no fall in the number of members of the Church of Scotland. Fewer set much store by regular attendance, but they still seek baptism, marriage and burial within the fold of the Church. As my own minister put it: "In practical living many may reject the religious view of life, but cannot quite accept all the implications of complete atheism."

Of course few attend church twice every Sunday as in the old days, but the churches are quite well filled—despite competing Sunday attractions and the fact that there is no stigma attached to non-attendance. Once a man's livelihood could depend upon attendance as is illustrated by the case of a factory owner in the South-west who broke away from the Kirk and set up a religious group of his own. Any of his employees who absented himself from the group's meetings on Sundays was called upon for an explanation the following day and if he repeated the offence he lost his job.

Nonetheless, the Church has problems, the greatest of which is the difficulty of finding suitable men to enter the ministry. Country boys are no longer attracted to the Kirk, and town-bred

7

Ploughing hillsides for new forests in Galloway
Mining, old style, at Waterside
Mining, new style, at Ochiltree

ministers do not always understand the problems of the country parishes well enough. I know of only one who remains close enough to the soil to graze the church glebe and attend market regularly.

On the other hand the growing industrialisation of parts of the South-west requires ministers who can develop the ministry to factories, schools and hospitals.

Finance, too, is a serious problem, for the days are gone when tierce payments took care of the minister's stipend and the heritors looked after the church property, so that the vast majority of the people contributed next to nothing. The attitude persists that the Church is somehow provided for, and that there is no need to give much money towards it. The days of the 'penny in the plate' should be over but many ministers would echo the words of the Ayrshire minister who quotes II Timothy 4 and 14—"Alexander the coppersmith did me much evil."

On the other hand one of his colleagues had a more direct approach to the matter. Sunday after Sunday he would fix his congregation with a defiant look, and say: "Freely have ye received; freely give. The collection will now be taken." By filling his lungs he could deliver the entire command (for such it was) without pause.

The Church remains the core of the life in the South-west. Some fifty years ago one went to church twice on a Sunday and that was the end of it until the following week. Now there is some activity centred on the Church every evening of the week—youth fellowship, Women's Guild, Men's Guild, badminton, drama, or some other social activity—which means that the Church premises are open every day of the week and religion is thought of as a thing for every day and not just for Sundays.

VI

HEROES OF SCOTLAND

BOOKS were scarce in the Burns household, and those to which Robert and his brother had access were greatly treasured. Among them was the story of Sir William Wallace, the hero of Scotland's fight for independence, whose memory is cherished the more because he died at the hands of the English—the painful death of a traitor to a sovereign to whom he had never even sworn allegiance.

Burns's imagination was fired by Wallace's association with Ayrshire, especially his own native district of Kyle, and as a youth he made many a pilgrimage to Leglen Woods, near Ayr, where Wallace had hidden nearly five centuries before. To an imaginative boy the deeds of Scotland's hero no doubt seemed as real as if they had taken place a mere five years earlier.

Wallace was not actually born in Ayrshire—his birthplace was Elderslie in Renfrewshire—but he had many kinsmen in Ayrshire, and was so closely linked with it that his enemies dubbed him 'King of Kyle'.

It is difficult to separate fact from fiction in Wallace's story for his chronicler, Blind Harry, was not one to spoil a story by the telling. And by the last quarter of the eighteenth century accuracy hardly mattered—it was all grist to Robert Burns's mill.

According to Blind Harry, Wallace first had to hide in Leglen Woods when he slew some English who came upon him as he fished the River Irvine at Riccarton near Kilmarnock and tried to steal his catch. From his refuge he made many adventurous forays into the enemy garrison town of Ayr, and one day Wallace accepted a wager from an Englishman who boasted that he could bear the hardest blow that any Scot could give him—as Blind Harry relates when Wallace struck him "the carle was dede". Another time Wallace was caught—overwhelmed by an enormous band of Englishmen—and thrown into prison. After a while he became so weak that the English thought he was dead, and left him lying outside the jail, where his old nurse found him and tended him back to health. The most frequently told tale, however, is that of the burning of the barns of Ayr, when a number of Scottish knights were lured to Ayr under guarantee of safe conduct and seized and hanged as they arrived. Wallace, who had returned home for the safe conduct which he had left behind, heard a rumour of the murder of his friends, and gathered together a force of men who set fire to the barns of Ayr with the English inside. Those who were able to flee the searing fire met swords hot with Wallace's anger, and not an Englishman escaped.

Wallace emerged from these escapades as leader of Scotland's fight against English domination and, although so much of his harrying of the enemy had taken place in Ayrshire, it was at Stirling Bridge in September 1297, that he defeated the English and made himself master of the country. His triumph lasted only ten months until he was beaten at Falkirk, and spent seven years as a fugitive until he was eventually captured and sent to London to be executed as a traitor in 1305. Wallace let Scotland taste freedom, and within months of his defeat at Falkirk another man had come forward to lead Scotland. His name was Robert Bruce, Earl of Carrick.

Bruce had a rival—John Comyn, known as the Red Comyn—who represented the Balliols, and became his bitter enemy. On 10th February 1306, Bruce and Comyn met in the Church of the Greyfriars in Dumfries and in a quarrel Bruce drew his dagger and stabbed Comyn. Running from the church Bruce cried, "I doubt I have slain the Red Comyn." "Doubt ye," answered Sir Roger

Kirkpatrick, "I'll mak' siccar",[1] and he entered the church and completed the deed. Like so much of the story of Scotland's heroes this *"I'll mak' siccar"* incident is probably apocryphal, if only for the reason given by Sir Herbert Maxwell that Kirkpatrick spoke Norman French and not Lowland Scots.

Whatever the truth of the tale; whatever the reason for the quarrel, the murder of the Red Comyn had one important outcome—it committed Bruce to fight for Scotland and set him on the road to Bannockburn. Six weeks later, on 25th March, Isabell, Countess of Buchan, set a simple circlet of Scottish gold on his head at Scone, and the Earl of Carrick became King Robert of Scotland.

Bruce's reign began inauspiciously. He was quickly defeated and forced to flee the country to wander abroad for a time until he landed eventually at Rathlin Island, off the northern coast of Ireland. From Rathlin the king moved on to Arran, where he was within easy reach of his native Carrick, and bided his time to return there. Carrick should have been full of friends, so Bruce instructed one of his men to cross over, spy out the land and light a fire if it was safe for the king to follow. The messenger found the district full of enemy soldiers and the local people apathetic, so he lit no fire. Nevertheless, the king did see a great blaze on the Carrick coast—probably only the burning of whins—and assumed that it was safe to return to the mainland.

First Bruce mauled the English garrison at Turnberry Castle; then he headed towards Hadyard Hill, a commanding position in the hills near Dailly, and set up camp there until he was forced to make for the shelter of the brown moors of Galloway. Like that period when Wallace hid in Leglen Woods, this was a time of heroism and treachery, of chases and ambushes laid by the Macdowalls of Garthland and other Gallovidians who had supported the Balliols and could not forgive Bruce for the murder of the Red Comyn. Among the lowering mountains in the wild, early months of 1307, Bruce fought brilliantly; his hairsbreadth escapes

[1] sure.

were as faithfully recorded by Barbour as those of Wallace were recounted by Blind Harry. In his great epic poem *The Bruce* Barbour told how the king was tracked by bloodhounds—once the enemy even set his own dog to trail him desperately over the moors to the south of Loch Doon, but when five soldiers caught up with Bruce, he and his brother Edward killed every one of them, and gained a few more hours. The pursuit was relentless as the faithful bloodhound searched for its master, and the king's danger increased. Barbour offers two endings to this tale. One tells how the king escaped by wading along a burn so that the dog lost his scent, and the other relates that Edward Bruce hid in the woods and shot the dog with an arrow as it passed by him.

With his brother and Sir James Douglas, Bruce fought back as fiercely as their enemies were relentless in their pursuit, and as so often happens it was the hunted who gained confidence—a confidence that increased with the first small victories. The turning point came at Glen Trool, when Bruce—a superb tactician—laid an ambush high on the Mulldonach hillside and rolled huge boulders on to the enemy, and then rushed down to scatter them. The Bruce Stone which stands high above the loch marks this victory at the Steps of Trool, which "opened the campaign of independence which he (Bruce) brought to a decisive close at Bannockburn".

Leaving his brother to continue the fight in Galloway, Bruce set out for other parts of Scotland to raise support. Edward Bruce fought battles near New Galloway (where the Cairn Edward Forest bears his name), and throughout Galloway to win the province for King Robert.

In the meantime Bruce, now sure of Carrick, Kyle and Cunningham, assured his hold on the South-west by another victory at Loudon Hill, but it took seven more years until Bannockburn was fought and Scotland's independence won at Midsummer, 1314.

The following year, the king called his parliament at Ayr to confirm his kingship, and settle the succession to the Scottish throne in case he should have no male heir. He did, indeed, have a son, who became David II, but the throne eventually went to the family of Bruce's daughter, Marjorie and Walter Steward—whose descendants were the unlucky Stewarts.

The story of Wallace and Bruce was just the material to inspire a boy with a vivid imagination like Robert Burns—as indeed they have inspired generations of less brilliant Scottish children since. If the details of the campaigns are obscure and we have forgotten the reasons behind the various moves in the War of Independence, the stories remain alive. Somewhere in the depths of my heart I can still feel the surge of national pride as I recall the Maister (as our village headmaster was known) recounting the tale of the burning of the barns of Ayr, or of Bruce's encounter with the determined spider of Rathlin, or of the fire which accidentally summoned him to save Scotland. It seems a pity that, beyond the primary school stage, Scottish history is so often left to become a mere extension of the history of England.

Nevertheless, in the formative years when history is little more than the exciting—and often apocryphal—tales of valiant men, it has the same effect as it had on young Robert Burns who said that Wallace's story "poured a Scottish prejudice into my veins which will boil among them till the floodgates of life shut in eternal rest".

Burns visited Falkirk, Bannockburn and Stirling, and no doubt as he stood where Scotland's freedom was defended and won, "Scottish prejudice" welled within him and he said "a fervent prayer for Old Caledonia". But it was neither Wallace nor Bruce that he commemorated in verse at Stirling. Burns had that Scottish whimsical yearning for the Jacobites which is so common even among the strongest opponents of Roman Catholicism, and among men whose forefathers fought for 'Butcher' Cumberland at Culloden or scoured the hills for Prince Charles Edward Stuart. The reason is no doubt, that they identify opposition to the Jacobites with the English, and in the century following the Union of the Parliaments of Scotland and England, many felt that they had lost that freedom which had been defended over so many centuries. The later Stuarts were unpopular in the Lowlands and would probably have been turned out by the Scots had the English not done so first. At any rate it was the Stuarts that Burns commemorated in Stirling when he took a diamond ring and scratched on a tavern window:

> The injured Stewart line is gone,
> A race outlandish fills their throne;
> An idiot race, to honour lost;
> Who know them best despise them most.

Burns was truly proud of Wallace and Bruce, but this pride did not result in a flow of patriotic verse lauding them. Rather did it sharpen his awareness of his own heritage in general terms so that he wanted to sing a song about his own folk instead of one about great men of the past; a ballad of the times in which he lived rather than one of long ago. Above all, he wanted to extol the beauty of his beloved Ayrshire, not of Scotland as a whole.

"I am hurt," he said, "to see other places of Scotland, their towns, rivers, woods, haughs, and etc., immortalised in such celebrated performances, whilst my dear native country, the ancient Baileries of Carrick, Kyle and Cunningham, famous both in ancient and modern times for a gallant and warlike race of inhabitants; a country where civil and particularly religious Liberty have ever found their first support, and their last asylum; a country, the birthplace of many famous Philosophers, Soldiers and Statesmen, and the scene of many important events recorded in Scottish history, particularly a great many of the actions of the glorious Wallace, the saviour of his Country; Yet, we have never had one Scottish poet of any eminence, to make the fertile banks of Irvine, the romantic woodlands and sequestered scenes of Ayr, and the heathy, mountainous source and winding sweep of Doon, emulate Tay, Forth, Ettrick, Tweed, and etc."

His heart longed to right this wrong, but modesty restrained him. "This complaint I would gladly remedy," he continued, "but alas I am far unequal to the task, both in native genius and education." He showed how wrong he was when he turned that very complaint into verse:

> Ramsay an' famous Fergusson
> Gied Forth an' Tay a lift aboon;
> Yarrow an' Tweed, to monie a tune,
> Owre Scotland rings;
> While Irwin, Lugar, Ayr, an' Doon,
> Naebody sings.

And when he had sung of these rivers so sweetly that it brought praise from another Ayrshire poet, Ochiltree schoolmaster, William Simson, he was able to reply:

> Auld Coila now may fidge fu' fain,
> She's gotten poets o' her ain;
> Chiels wha their chanters winna hain[1],
> But tune their lays,
> Till echoes a' resound again
> Her weel-sung praise.

Although Robert Burns determined to write about (and for) his own folk he did not forget Wallace's deeds. In that same "Epistle to William Simson", he wrote:

> At Wallace's name, what Scottish blood
> But boils up in a spring-tide flood!
> Oft have our fearless fathers strode
> By Wallace' side,
> Still pressing onward, red-wat-shod,
> Or glorious died!

And the Wars of Independence produced the moving song of "Bruce Before Bannockburn", which rings today as Scotland's

[1] spare.

national anthem, ranking second in popularity only to "Auld Lang Syne". There never was a finer rallying call than:

> Scots, wha hae wi' Wallace bled,
> Scots, wham Bruce has aften led,
> Welcome to your gory bed,
> Or to victorie.

And yet, was he not rallying men to fight for freedom and overthrow tyranny in his own time as much as in Bruce's? Was he thinking of 1314 or of troubled Scotland of the 1790s, when those who fought for social reform banded themselves into the 'Friends of the People', and the London Government ruthlessly retaliated by bringing a group led by Thomas Muir to trial and deporting them to the Australian colonies? Contemporary problems must have been in Burns's mind when he wrote:

> By oppression's woes and pains!
> By your sons in servile chains!
> We will drain our dearest veins,
> But we shall be free!

"Scots Wha Hae" is a timeless plea for liberty. As such it has become especially dear to freedom-loving Scots, and if Robert Burns had not written another line of poetry "Scots Wha Hae" would have made him great. We should be grateful for the inspiration these heroes of Scotland were to Burns, just as we ought to be thankful that people like his mother and old Betty Davidson gave him the tongue to express himself.

Thanks to them he made the resolve:

> We'll sing auld Coila's plains an' fells,
> Her moors red-brown wi' heather bells,
> Her banks an' braes, her dens and dells,
> Where glorious Wallace
> Aft bure the gree[1], as story tells,
> Frae Suthron Billies.

[1] carried the prize.

Thanks to them he carried out that resolve so that Kyle and its modest rivers became immortalised as few other places in the world have been:

> O sweet are Coila's haughs an' woods,
> When lintwhite chant amang the buds,
> And jinkin hares, in amorous whids[1],
> Their loves enjoy;
> While thro' the braes the cushat croods[2]
> With wailfu' cry!

[1] leaps.
[2] pigeon coos.

VII

THESE ARE THE PEOPLE

THE heroes of Scotland, the medieval feuds, and the grim fight of
the Covenanters have all helped to make the South-western Scot
the man he is today. Equally, he has been influenced by a con-
tinuous struggle to scrape a living from soil that was cold, wet and
sour. This last was the influence that shaped Burns's life more than
any other, and of course it was the terrible weight that bore down
on him before he had time to sing all the glorious songs which
lilted in his mind. Life in Scotland is easier today, for the soil is
well improved and machinery has been invented to lighten some
of the harder tasks, but the farmer's life is a strenuous one even
now. The dairy farmer still rises between five and six in the
morning and works with little rest until the evening milking is
over, which is sometime after six. At harvest time he must return
to the fields even then to gather his crop while the weather holds.

John R. Allan, himself a farmer in the North-east, knows just
how hard life is on Ayrshire farms. In his book *Summer in Scotland*
he tells of an Aberdeenshire farmer who wished to interview an
Ayrshire dairyman, so he went early to make sure he did not miss
him. It was six o'clock and still dark when he arrived at the farm,
and asked for the dairyman.

"O what a pity you're so late, he's away," they told him.

"Late?" the Aberdeenshire man was just able to say.

"O yes," they replied. "You see, the master left *in the morning*."

It reminds me of my father who used to bustle into the kitchen for tea about mid-morning and exclaim: "Ten o'clock. Anither day by and no' a damn hate[1] done." Of course, he had done five hours' work by that time. On reflection, that was one of the chief reasons why I did not follow in his footsteps; I never could have risen at that hour.

It is a hard life, and it has toughened the people. Even those in the towns are not far from the influences of the countryman's struggle, for apart from the three towns of Ayr, Kilmarnock and Dumfries, this is essentially a rural community. And even these three towns owe so much of their existence to agriculture that their outlook is rural.

To the toughness has been added a determination and certainty which goes beyond dourness to obstinacy—or to use a dialect word which takes it a step further, *essertness*. Again this is traceable to the religious fight of the seventeenth century when men had to be prepared to die for their beliefs, and that meant they had to be sure of them. For that reason, the Ayrshire or Galloway man does not make up his mind lightly, and, having made it up, he will not change it.

Most dour of all are the men of Kyle where one can sometimes meet with a degree of obstinacy that could lead to such heartrending human tragedies as are described in George Douglas Brown's novel *The House With The Green Shutters*. It has been suggested that Brown was exaggerating when he described Ochiltree—Barbie of the book; Dougall in his *Burns Country*, for example, says: "The spiteful back-biting, the overbearing ignorance, the snivelling hypocrisy, and the brutish insensibility to pain, which form the atmosphere of Barbie do not belong to Ochiltree."

Don't they? True, it is unfair to single out Ochiltree—or any other village—but such people exist in Kyle as I should know for one half of my family tree grew there. I know of families who have quarrelled so that when brothers met at market they ignored

[1] thing.

one another and the family home and inheritance were handed out of the family. Another farmer cut his daughter off without even the proverbial shilling, because she married one of the hired men on the farm.

It takes hard men to do such things.

Generally speaking, however, Kyle folk are as happy, kindly and friendly as anywhere in Scotland, and to strangers they are generosity and courtesy itself. Yet strangely enough, it is among their own families that their quarrelsomeness is most in evidence.

Ayr itself, is never dull; nevertheless it seems to have lost much of the gaiety for which it was known in Burns's time. Recalling his youth about the beginning of the nineteenth century, Lord Cockburn wrote of the town: "It was then . . . filled with the families of gentlemen—from the county, from India, and from public service; and was a gay, card-playing, dancing, scandal-loving place. There seemed to be a dinner, or a tea and card party every day at several houses of Kennedys and Boswells and Crawfords and Dalrymples; lots of old colonels and worthy old ladies; and to get up a ball, nothing was wanted but for somebody to suggest it, and they would be footing it away in a few hours."

The aristocracy may no longer 'foot it away' in Ayr, but the town remains a bright place, and its people enjoy themselves, even without the sophistication of city ways. Although Ayr is so close to Glasgow it has been able to retain its essential atmosphere of the smaller town.

Burns gave Ayr a reputation to live up to when he wrote:

> Auld Ayr wham ne'er a toun surpasses
> For honest men, and bonnie lasses.

As early as 1844 Cockburn cast doubts on the accuracy of this. "I find Ayr still boasts of its female beauty . . .", he wrote, "but though on the lookout, I can't say my eyes were particularly dazzled." He passes no comment on the honesty of the men, although he should have been in a better position than most to do so.

South of the Doon the character of the people begins to change, for this is the land of Tam O'Shanter, or rather of Douglas Graham, the Kirkoswald farmer who inspired the poem. In my youth we had a Tam O'Shanter in the district whom I shall call James Smith, although that is not his real name. Like Tam O'Shanter, James frequently "sat boozing at the nappie" in Ayr, and made his way home, by some obscure guidance, in the early hours. These were the times of food shortage, when farmers had to be on the alert for poultry thieves around Christmas, and James raised frequent false alarms when he drove his old car into a farmyard in order to gather his scattered wits before continuing his journey home. Whether or not he ever saw a 'cutty sark' on any of these occasions is not recorded.

Carrick is more isolated than the other parts of Ayrshire, and the dour hand of civilisation has neither marred the natural gaiety of the people nor given them the city man's inhibitions. There is little manufacturing industry, so the people remain essentially the product of a rural society—even the miners of the Dailly district are countrymen at heart and in outlook. This characteristic is continued right out of Carrick into Wigtownshire where the leavening of Irish blood makes its contribution to the make-up of the people.

With this carefree couthiness comes a reputation of which there is little to boast. Around Maybole they have a reputation for poaching, and in Carrick generally they have the highest illegitimacy rate for the county, about ten per cent above the Ayrshire average. In Wigtownshire the figure rises even higher, and as a young journalist in Glasgow, I remember the regularity with which we received a report of the latest addition to one unmarried mother's brood in Wigtownshire. She held the record for the country—something like twelve or thirteen illegitimate children, I think—and seemed proud of the fact.

Kirkcudbright and Ayrshire folk tend to consider themselves a cut above their Wigtownshire neighbours. One man in the Stewartry told me that when any school reports a problem child to him, it invariably turns out to be an incomer from Wigtownshire. Wigtownshire people do not appear to take life as seriously as others do and, although many of them are less richly endowed than their neighbours in more industrially advanced parts, they possess a natural warmth and charm which far outshines many of their fellow Scots.

In the Stewartry and Dumfriesshire the people resemble Ayrshire folk—which is as it should be for there is a goodly infusion of Ayrshire blood in their veins. However, as one moves eastward into the Border country the character becomes more sharply defined, probably through centuries of living in that uneasy frontier land between Scotland and England. Perhaps it is from this environment that the Dumfriesian derives a closeness which can puzzle strangers. The true Dumfriesian does not put all his cards on the table in his dealings with incomers until he has had time to size them up, and even then he is apt to remain close. Even on the least important matters he gives little away, and will tell you that he was visiting friends last night, but will not mention their name, although he knows that they are mutual friends. A Dumfriesian who has lived outside the Queen of the South for many years comments: "It is a curious trait, and the motive is often far from plain, so that it could become irritating if one allowed it to."

Burns had little to say about the inhabitants of Dumfries, although he did write on occasion that he "finds the people quite charming". John Home, the author of *Douglas* liked them too, and said so in verse:

> Thy people's manners my affections move;
> They win my numbers who engage my love,
> Industrious are thy sons, yet free and fair;
> Though busy cheerful; and though wise, sincere;
> Fair are thy maids—too fair for hearts like mine;
> Careless, they please, and charm without design;
> By sense conducted, neither fond nor coy,
> But made for modest love and sober joy.

Scotland ends at the Mull of Galloway

Robert Heron was rather more critical when he made his journey through the western counties of Scotland in 1792. He found the town "a place of higher gaiety and elegance than any other town in Scotland of the same size", and the mode of living of the people "rather shewy than luxurious".

"The citizens of Dumfries are frugal of their money," he wrote, "but hold idleness a proof of gentility: and they value only such enjoyments as they can be seen to share, and can be esteemed the greater for sharing. They delight in fine and fashionable clothes."

How has the town changed? In appearance it looks prosperous and well kept, although that end associated with Burns for some years looked battered and crumbling, but is now being improved. The people are neither mean nor self-seeking, as Heron asserts. Dumfries is a friendly town, and it is appropriate that the annual civic festival should be named Guid Nychburris (Good Neighbours).

The character of the South-western Scot in every part—Wigtown and Dumfries, Ayr and Kirkcudbright alike—is overlaid by reserve and caution which gives the Sassenach the impression that he is stilted and reserved. Nevertheless, every visitor makes the same comment about him—his generosity and kindly warmheartedness shine through the veneer of native caution. The Scots themselves have a word for it—couthiness. Folk of the South-west are warm-hearted to strangers, and open-handed to their own in times of need.

In the first Statistical Account of Scotland published during Burns's lifetime, the minister of the parish of Kirkmichael in Dumfriesshire related how when disaster threatened to engulf one of his parishioners, the community would hold what it called a Drinking. The unfortunate parishioner supplied beer, bread and cheese, and the whole community gathered to dance and enjoy his hospitality. To participate everyone contributed a shilling or more, so that at the end of the evening the needy person would be £5 or more the richer.

I asked a minister in the Stewartry about this trait in his
8

Ailsa Craig dominates the Firth of Clyde
Portpatrick—now a quiet holiday resort

parishioners. "You know," he replied, "generosity often comes from the most unexpected quarters. More than once a farmer who might be considered a bit mean has handed me a sum of money for some member of the community who was in need. And always he will add, 'But dinna tell him where it came from'."

Like true Scots the South-westerners are proud people who respect men for what they are rather than for any office they may hold. They do not feel subservient to men who are richer or more highly educated than they are. After all every family in Scotland, however humble, has its professional men—sons who have gone to university to become doctors, ministers or teachers—so that they are quite familiar with education and do not stand in awe of it. In my home, which was a typical Ayrshire farmhouse, the next person to call might be an earl or a roadmender, but whoever he was, he received the same welcome, tea out of the same pot, or (in better times) whisky from the same bottle. From time to time the two arrived simultaneously and then, instead of manoeuvring them apart, one simply let them meet on equal terms. Ayrshire folk may have their peers, but not their betters.

Despite all that is said about the Scotsman's reverence for education, there is today a kind of mental inertia pervading the whole of Scotland, and this prompts the question, "Stands Scottish education where it did?" In the Statistical Account of the Parish of Ochiltree, published in 1951, it was reported: "Neither parents nor children seem to care much about school work." Love of learning and desire for betterment are the qualities which made Scotland great; one can only hope that they will never vanish, for if they do, this country will lose the richest heritage of any nation.

There is some reassurance in the comment of an Ayrshire schoolmaster on the subject. "It is fair comment," he said, "that a considerable section of the community is against any form of discipline or authority, but one must bear in mind that the Scottish tradition of sending one member of the family to a university is as strong today as it was between and before the two World Wars.

THESE ARE THE PEOPLE

Just think of your own little corner of Ayrshire and the number of University graduates it has produced."

Of course he is right; education still means much to the Scot, especially to the rural section of the community. Others may be different—the miners, for example, have more radical and more militant traditions, but they, too, have produced their quota of Great Scots.

The Scot in general, and the South-western Scot in particular, hates humbug and cant. Airs and graces are loathsome to him and he tends to scorn that which he does not understand. Even in his speech there is a kind of inverted snobbery, so that he uses what he fondly believes to be the Doric, when all he is doing is speaking bad English with a Scottish accent. One frequently hears him say "*the night*" for 'tonight', when he ought to say "*the nicht*" if he wanted to use the Scottish tongue. The last Statistical Account observed this trait in the Parish of Dalrymple: "Perhaps the greatest cultural shortcoming is that of speech. The old vernacular is almost extinct, and has been replaced by a debased and slovenly form of English."

On the other hand, he sometimes has good reason for scorn—often his fellows believe it is vulgar to use the Doric and they assume a bastard English accent. This happened in Minishant when a youth of the village went south for a few weeks to visit a relative and returned with an English accent. On hearing him one of the worthies of the village hurried to her neighbour (and confidante) with the horrified exclamation: "Declare tae God, ye wad think he had cut his lip on an English chanty."[1] Not that she despised him for using educated talk—it was the 'English' accent to which she took exception. On more than one occasion she herself violated the Oxford Dictionary. When a lost sheep was found hungry and emaciated, she related the incident to her neighbour, ending with the exclamation, "Declare tae God, the puir beast was starvin'. It was the maist emancipated sheep I ever saw."

It was this same villager, who, commenting on another youth

[1] chamber pot.

who swore loudly and frequently, deplored his language and summed him up with a withering sentence: "Declare tae God, he's the damndest swearer."

The language of the Scot in the South-west is still colourful, for there are still some of the 'damndest swearers' in evidence, but his voice is slow, flat and tending to be monotonous. Vowels are extended interminably so that one becomes impatient to finish a word or sentence for him, and this drawling speech is well illustrated by friends' greeting to my mother when she visits them. Those who use her pet name, Tot (pronounced to rhyme with boat) invite her in, and say: "Can I take your coat, Tot?"—every vowel lovingly lingering on the tip of their tongue so that it sounds rather like: "*Caan aah taak' yer cote, Tote?*"

Carrick marks the barrier where the pace of the speech quickens and vowels shorten so that '*blaack*' in Ayr becomes '*bluck*' in Maybole. From this point south the voices take on a more Irish intonation until Wigtownshire is reached and the speech becomes similar to that of Northern Ireland. Indeed, it is often referred to as Galloway Irish. In Carrick and Galloway the consonants become more liquid—the *l* especially comes near to the French pronounciation, and the *t* either vanishes altogether or is softened to *th*.

Although dialect is rare among the middle classes in the Burns Country it still clings tenaciously among the ordinary folk in both country and town. It was feared that the radio might ruin the Scottish tongue, but about forty years of broadcasting has done little more than encroach on it. Undoubtedly the constant reminder of our great-great-grandfathers' voice through poems of Burns is an important influence in the retention of dialect, and most people are bilingual. The working man speaks modified standard English at school, to the minister, the doctor, and so on, but he retains his own rich vernacular for conversation among his family and neighbours. The middle classes speak modified standard English all the time, but understand dialect perfectly well. The upper classes are educated in England so their speech is wholly English, although they, too, understand the vernacular.

Among ordinary men—the man in the 'stubble' field, so to speak—speech remains basically that of Robert Burns and his contemporaries, even if a large number of dialect words have vanished. Language is constantly changing and, having accepted, as we must, that change is inevitable we should be thankful that in speech (as in character) the people of the Burns Country are much the same today as they were two hundred years ago, when the youth following the plough on Lochlie was not just another Kyle man, but Robert Burns, Scotland's bard-to-be.

VIII

ON AYRSHIRE SOIL . . .

Throughout South-west Scotland the people are countrymen whose industry and recreation revolves round the seasons, the soil and its harvest. Even those townsmen whose livelihood is derived from manufacturing industry remain close to the land.

Agriculture is the cornerstone of the economy, and the farmer is the mainstay of the population. But just as the generation just passing has wrought change, so too did the generation in which Burns lived. The late eighteenth century was a period of great progress in agriculture, but this improvement was achieved at the cost of much distress to thousands of people who were driven into the towns as the land was parcelled into larger holdings. Today similar upheavals are taking place, for farms which have been run by families for generations are now being taken over by a new gentry who have no traditional connection with the land. On a family farm in the old days the farmer and his sons were responsible for the outside work, while his wife and daughters kept house, looked after the hens, and helped in the dairy. The egg money was the traditional 'perk' of the women, and many farmhouses have been furnished from the proceeds of the sale of eggs. The henhouse has also dressed many a farmer's daughter—and dressed her well.

As families reduced in size outside help had to be brought in to run the family farms, and labour costs added to increasing running costs generally and lack of capital to mechanise made these farms uneconomic to run. Furthermore, rising land prices made it impossible for these farmers to set their sons up in farms when the time came, so farms began to be bought up by wealthy industrialists from the towns who fancied themselves in the role of weekend lairds. The process has continued until today many farms are in the possession of the shooting-stick lairds who, although they have spent large sums of money on their farms, have neither the knowledge nor the interest in the land which their predecessors had.

The form of agriculture varies according to the soil and the size of holding. On the coast of Ayrshire and Wigtownshire, where the soil is sandy and light, early potatoes are grown for the markets of central Scotland. The shore farmers know good potatoes and, although older folk will complain that potatoes have little taste today compared with the time when less artificial fertiliser was used, the Epicures which are the first early potatoes of Ayrshire are firm and sweet.

Inland the soil becomes heavier and grain and root crops replace 'early tatties'. However, few farms are devoted solely to cropping —almost everywhere there is a herd of dairy cows as well. Despite an increase in the raising of beef cattle which are more profitable and require less attention, one cannot drive far along a country road about four o'clock on a summer's afternoon without meeting the cows being herded home for evening milking. Collies nip their heels, but the cows refuse to be hurried, and pause in their progress to cast a haughty look over vehicle and driver. These dairy cows are brown and white, for this is the home of the Ayrshire, a breed belonging to Kyle and Cunningham, but common throughout the Machars of Wigtownshire, the Stewartry of Kirkcudbright, and the county of Dumfries. An Ayrshire man will tell you that these are the finest dairy cattle in the world; the Jersey may give richer milk and the Friesian more of it, but the Ayrshire's quality milk and all-round handsome looks have won it frequent triumphs at the Royal Dairy Show in London. As a judge of the breed put it:

One is impressed with the broad muzzle, the sweet, open, clear eye, showing a mild temperament, the flat crown and a moderately sized horn, finishing up with smart well-carried ears.

That is the Ayrshire cow—a lady popular in almost every part of the world.

The Ayrshire cow has its own fan club, the Ayrshire Cattle Society, whose offices are in Ayr.

Dairying has changed in the past generation. Once the cows produced generously in summer only, and stood unproductive in the byre throughout the winter, so that there was an enormous surplus of milk at certain times of the year, which had to be turned into butter and cheese on the farm. Nowadays production is more evenly distributed over the year, and the milk is collected by the Scottish Milk Marketing Board, to be processed at creameries.

Home production of butter and cheese had almost ceased by the early 1930s, and I have only a vague recollection of the great vats of curd on our farm. However, I remember the decaying cheese presses—*chissets*, they were called—lying in the barn, and the curd vats serving as containers for cattle feed. We still have the wooden blocks used for printing the butter with designs which tended to run to clover leaves, thistles and stars, and there is one of which we are especially proud because it bears my father's name and address round its circumference.

When the land rises the soil becomes thinner, and the grass loses its lushness, so that hardy beef cattle replace dairy cows. Here the South-west has contributed a breed whose name is known all over the world—the shaggy-coated Galloway, which is reputed to have been introduced by the Norsemen. Whatever the truth of that, the Galloway thrives on bleak hillsides both here and in overseas countries. The breed, which has its own Society at Castle Douglas, enjoys such popularity that in a recent year more of them were exported from the United Kingdom than of any other breed —beef or dairy. And in 1964 Galloways won every major championship at the Royal Smithfield Show in London.

Sharing the hill pastures with Galloway cattle, and venturing to even bleaker heights, are hardy Blackfaced sheep, although in many places they are being ousted to make way for new forests which are being planted through much of the Province, often on land which could easily support sheep. In autumn the sheep are brought to milder lowland farms to graze while dairy cows are lying indoors for the winter. Hill farmers often send their sheep to the same lowland pastures year after year, and the day in mid-October when the winterers arrive is an important one. The throaty groan of laden lorries accompanied by an unaccustomed bleating of sheep announces their arrival, and the lowland dogs are beside themselves with excitement. When the hill sheep arrive the winter routine begins, with regular forays—often on Sunday mornings—to 'look the winterers'. Times have changed and the inspection of the hill sheep is often made by tractor instead of on foot.

The use of the tractor and all the mechanical equipment that accompanies it is another part of the agrarian revolution of our time, and it has resulted in the virtual disappearance of the handsome Clydesdale horse which was once bred in large numbers in the South-west of Scotland. Most farmers in these parts have a great love for horses and on our farm, as on many others, a few were retained long after their work had been taken over by the tractor. Perhaps the animal which my father loved more than any other in his entire farming life, was his stallion Coronation, which was as precious to him as if he had been that greatest Clydesdale of all time, the *Baron of Buchlyvie*.

The Baron was bred at the beginning of the present century at Buchlyvie in Stirlingshire, but he was the subject of a dispute over ownership between two of the great Ayrshire horse breeders, James Kilpatrick of Craigie Mains at Kilmarnock, and William Dunlop of Dunure Mains, near Ayr. The quarrel was taken to the House of Lords before it was finally decided that the Baron was the joint property of the two men. And when the owners agreed in 1911 to sell the Baron his fame was so great that a crowd of four or five thousand gathered at Ayr Market to witness the sale.

Apart from a jesting offer of half-a-crown from an Ayr farmer the bidding settled down to a duel between the joint owners until Kilpatrick withdrew and left Dunlop the sole owner of the horse. The price was £9,500, the highest ever paid for a draught horse of any breed, and a staggering figure by 1911 standards. No wonder Dunlop described the Baron a quarter of a century later as "a sensational and bewitching horse". The end of the story of the Baron of Buchlyvie is a sad one; he died only three years later as a result of a kick on the foreleg from a mare.

In many ways the story of the Baron of Buchlyvie is as much a comment on the breed of farmers in the South-west as on the breed of their animals. They are a hardy race—industrious, shrewd and determined men, unwilling to relinquish what they believe to be their rights.

Although they are in many ways slow to accept change the farmers in the area support one of the country's greatest centres of agricultural education, the Glasgow and West of Scotland Agricultural College, which is located at Auchincruive, the former home of the Wallaces who were kinsmen of Sir William Wallace. Appropriately, it was an Ayrshire man, Robert Patrick Wright, who founded the college, and became its first Principal. Wright was born at Downan, near Ballantrae in 1857, and before he was thirty years old he had been appointed Professor and Director of the Agricultural Department of the Glasgow and West of Scotland Technical College. In Ayrshire, however, landlords and tenant farmers of the South-west had set up their Scottish Dairy Institute, and it was a fusion of this institute with Wright's department in Glasgow that established the West of Scotland Agricultural College. A well-known Ayrshire farmer, John Hannah of Girvan Mains presented the estate of Auchincruive to the college, and it is on that estate that a farm, a dairy school, a poultry school, an apiary and a horticultural department are located.

The College, and its close links with the local farming community, prove that the farmer of the South-west is not averse to

progress—even if he does appear to accept it slowly until its worth
has been proved. The gift of Auchincruive is typical of the
generosity of these same farmers, and the good use they make of
the knowledge of the college staff in the running of their farms
and solving of their day-to-day problems, shows their shrewdness.

Burns gave us glimpses of the farmer and cotter of his time.
Other poets have shown us the farmers of our own day. David
Ramsay, who knew the farming community well and whose wife
was the daughter of a tenant farmer, wrote this epitaph to his
friend 'Toonie', Thomas Robertson of Townhead of Drumley;
he might have been writing of a hundred other farmers in the
neighbourhood:

> Maist mornin's then he beat the lark;
> I've seen him, strippet tae the sark,
> Hard at it tae, lang efter dark
> > Wi' beasts tae feed;
> On Ayrshire soil there's left a mark
> > Though 'Toonie's' deid.

That is life on the land; it is much the same on the sea. Down
the coast of Ayrshire, round the beetling Mull of Galloway, and
on along the drunken indentations of the Solway coast lie
villages and ancient seaports from which Scottish vessels once
sailed to markets overseas and especially to the New World. Dumfries, Kirkcudbright, Ayr and Irvine were important seaports
from which much trade was conducted, and from which many
emigrants sailed to the colonies. Indeed, it was from Kirkcudbright that ships sailed under Sir William Alexander of Menstrie
to found Scotland's first ill-starred colony in the New-Found-
Land of America. After Burns's time Portpatrick grew to be the
packet station for the Irish Channel crossing, but it was superseded
by Stranraer a century ago and dwindled in importance. In time
Glasgow and the ports close to it overtook the more distant ones
of the South-west so that only Ayr, Irvine, Troon and Ardrossan
have much trade now.

While the seaports were engrossed in their honest mercantile pursuits, the smaller coves along the coast were prosperous centres of smuggling. Burns encountered the 'riot and swagger' of those who indulged in the trade when he spent some time at Kirkoswald, an inland village but near enough to Maidens and Dunure to feel the influence of the smugglers. Alas, life is much more respectable on the coast these days and it is doubtful if a sixpenny worth of smuggling takes place today, but the coves of Dunure, Maidens, Ballantrae and so on retain their link with the sea through their fishing fleets.

For centuries fishermen have lived hereabouts, leading a hard, isolated life which has moulded them into an introspective race, who stand apart from all others in the region. Their mode of fishing and the danger of their calling has welded them into a community much more closely knit than any other, and for generations they have been independent of outsiders, yet dependent on one another. Families have intermarried so that the same surnames are encountered in the villages over many generations— McCreaths, McCrindles, Sloans and Girvans.

Like fishermen anywhere, they were—and are—at the mercy of the fickle elements, the success of the catch, and the price which they may be offered for it. Of course, progress has ameliorated the harsh life. Motor boats have largely replaced sailing vessels, so that the men can venture to the Hebrides and round Scotland to the North Sea fishing grounds. These boats are equipped with radar, echo-sounding gear and two-way radios, which make for greater safety and larger hauls at the expense of less effort. Netting, too, brings larger catches, and eliminates the long night's work of baiting lines for a dawn start in the old days. And, of course, sounder marketing methods, with an assurance that surplus fish will be bought for processing into fish meal, makes for financial stability.

Nonetheless, this is no easy way of earning a living. Fishing is still a man's calling—it is a pursuit for independent spirits who do not want office hours and feather-bed conditions. The fishermen spend long periods away from home, and they still receive their remuneration by the old fashioned apportioning of the payment received for the catch—several portions awarded to the boat and gear, and one for each of the members of the crew.

Although the fisherman is different from the rest of the community a new factor is changing his life rapidly, and that is the growth of the tourist industry. Holidaymakers have brought new life and prosperity to fishing villages and towns which seemed a few years ago to be on the point of dying. Girvan, for example, is a thriving holiday resort to which the fishing boats and the net-menders seem little more than a picturesque backcloth. In seaside villages gaily painted cottages display 'Bed and Breakfast' signs to attract the touring motorist, and many of these places are ringed with caravans which mar their appearance to those who knew them before the tourists arrived. At Maidens, for example, caravans cover almost as large an area as the village itself and even the embankment which once carried the Carrick shore railway is lined with caravans.

One would not grudge the holidaymakers the pleasure which these lovely villages bring them, nor can one deny the fisherfolk a little easily earned money, but one thinks of what has happened along the North Wales coast, and hopes that the same fate will not befall the Clyde or Solway shores.

The third major outdoor industry of the South-west is forestry, which does not employ a large number of workers although it takes up many square miles of upland country. The story of state afforestation in the South-west really begins in the years after the First World War when a start was made on the shores of Loch Ken; a slow, painstaking start, for the work of preparation and planting was carried out manually. Now mechanisation has come to forestry, and great tractor-drawn ploughs turn over furrows such as Gulliver might have discovered in Brobdignag. These furrows drain the land and make it easy to insert the trees by hand, an operation which I always feel must be performed by men who have a touching belief in the future, for few of them will actually see the harvest of their planting.

In the forests of the South-west a number of varieties of trees are grown, among them stately Douglas firs, the Christmas tree Sitka Spruce, the Norway Spruce, the Larch and the Scots Pine, each of them producing a different type of timber suited to a different purpose.

The yield of these forests which run through Ayrshire and Galloway to Dumfriesshire, is already considerable—close on two million cubic feet of timber per annum from the state forests of the South-west alone. This output will rise to seven million cubic feet a year by 1980. Add to this impressive figure the one-and-three-quarter million cubic feet from private estates at present, with a promise of future increase and one begins to see the dimension of this industry.

Such output takes one a long way from a few trees beside Loch Ken. The Forestry Commission and the Department of Agriculture and Fisheries for Scotland control 143,000 acres of forest, and another 50,000 acres are in private hands. Yet all these acres employ only about 1,100 men, more or less equally divided between private and state forests.

New villages were built to house forestry workers at Ae (the shortest placename in Scotland) and at Glen Trool, both of which were experiments in placing a new community in the country close to the forests and both of them launched with a great beating of drums. Although each village now comprises some fifty houses and the population of each is around two hundred, the tendency today is to integrate forestry workers' houses into existing villages, and there are sizeable communities of these men and their families in the villages of Barr, New Galloway and Minnigaff.

The future of forestry is hard to define, for there are some who claim that it has already encroached too far on to land which ought to support sheep. The answer is to establish a proper balance between the use of land for trees or sheep, and unfortunately it is not an easy answer to find.

However much one may dispute land use, one point is beyond all controversy—the forests have created an outstanding recreational amenity without which Scotland would be poor, indeed. In the great forest park of Glen Trool more than 100,000 acres of land are open to climbers, walkers, naturalists and to those who just want to contemplate the fierce beauty of mountain, loch and river. This is land for the energetic, with hillpaths which are a challenge to the stoutest heart. It is also land for those who take their pleasures more leisurely. Andrew McCormick, who lives in Galloway and loves it better than almost anyone, wrote in the Forestry Commission's Guide to Glen Trool:

> Our mountains are suited for anyone who is an average walker, and is sound in wind and limb, especially for anyone who likes leisurely to ascend by the easiest route and spend the whole day rambling along a range of mountains with glorious prospects of colourful moorland and grand hills all around. Then there are the lovely glens running into the uplands for those who no longer aspire to reach the summit—and who may derive much consolation from Schopenhauer, who said that "a church is best viewed from the outside, a public house from the inside and a mountain from the foot".

The opening up of the state forests to the holidaymaker and nature lover has brought the greatest hazard of all to the forests, namely fire. Here and there in the larger forests great fire breaks have been made between sections of forest, and these can be seen from the road, running like huge scars along the hillsides. Water tanks, look-out towers, brooms to beat out fires and constant warning notices all serve to remind the traveller of the risk of fire. Nevertheless it is the fire which picnickers fail to smother and the carelessly dropped cigarette end that constitutes the greatest danger to the new forests. In summer a blaze can race through hundreds of trees and destroy years of work within minutes. At the same time it ruins the great social amenity of forest parks.

IX

A SEPARATE AND AVOIDED TRIBE

THE coalminer is the link between country and town-based industry in South-west Scotland. Although none of the mining centres are much more than overgrown villages and pithead and farmstead stand in juxtaposition, the produce of the coalmine is so closely linked with industry that it probably belongs more truly to the chapter on urban industry.

Coal-mining has been associated with the South-west of Scotland for many centuries, and a Crossraguel Abbey charter dating from 1415 refers to the existence of coal heughs at Dailly. This does not mean that mining began only then; it must date much further back although we have no proof of earlier working of coal.

It was two and a half centuries after that 1415 charter that mining was first undertaken on a large scale in Ayrshire. In the north of the county, at Stevenston, Sir George Cunningham sank a coalmine, and built a harbour at Saltcoats from which to export the coal, mainly to Ireland. Although mining continued throughout the eighteenth century in the northern end of the county, it was the coming of the railways towards the middle of the nineteenth century that brought the development of the coalfields of central and southern Ayrshire, until mines stretched from under the sea off the coast at Prestwick right over the county boundary to Sanquhar in Dumfriesshire, and from the Garnock Valley in the north to the Girvan Valley in the south. The pits produced—and

Machars landscape is wild and wind-swept

still do produce—grand coal, suited to all the markets, household, industrial and power stations, although the seams are not always easily worked. Often they lie deep in the earth, sometimes they are broken by geological faults, and here and there they are thin and irregular. The deepest mine in the South-west is at Killoch Colliery, which has a shaft 2,490 feet deep.

Despite the difficulties of mining Ayrshire coal, the industry grew rapidly in the nineteenth century, but it has not spoiled the beauty of the best of the countryside. Indeed, travelling about the county, one is scarcely aware of the existence of the mines, even in the heart of the Burns Country. Fortunately, the worst of the scarring of the landscape has taken place in the remoter parts of the county out of sight of the tourist.

Two great companies worked much of the coal—William Baird and Company and the Dalmellington Iron Company, and the merging of these in the 1930s formed a powerful coalmining interest which existed until nationalisation at the end of the Second World War.

Since nationalisation, changes have taken place. Mining methods have been modernised, unproductive pits have been closed, and productive ones expanded. The number of pits has fallen from thirty-five in 1947 to fourteen, and the number of men employed has also dropped from 12,750 to something over 6,000. The output of saleable coal has decreased in that time from just over three and a half million tons to just over two million tons.

The need to maintain the size of the coal pieces for sale to the household market together with practical difficulties due to geological faulting has made it difficult to mechanise the mines in this part of Scotland as easily as elsewhere. However, more than two-thirds of the coal is power-loaded nowadays.

And what of the men who dig the coal? Like the farmers and fishermen, they stand out sharply from their fellows, which is not surprising when one considers the traditions and background of the mining community. Like most of my countrymen I can remember being taught that 1833 was an important date because

"The toil-worn Cotter frae his labour goes"

that was the year in which slavery was abolished. But no-one taught me that 1799 was equally important, because in that year slavery was abolished in my own country, and that those last slaves were the miners and the salters.

In 1606 the Scottish Parliament passed a disgraceful Act condemning the colliers and salters to slavery. *The History of The Scottish Coal-mining Industry* published by the Scottish Division of the National Coal Board explains:

At all costs the collier must be kept to the coal-heughs! His position under the new Act differed from that of the slave only in that his master had not the power to bring him out of the mine and dispose of him by public auction in the marketplace. The opening up of new collieries had led the new owners, having no trained workmen of their own, to entice experienced workmen from established collieries by means of gifts and promises of higher wages. This was strongly resented by their former masters, and in the Act of 1606 it was ordained that no person should fee, hire or conduce (take away) any salters, colliers or coalbearers without a written authority from the master whom they had last served; otherwise their former masters could reclaim them 'within a year and a day' and the colliers or coalbearers who had accepted wages from their new masters were to be regarded as thieves and punished accordingly. In 1641 the Act was extended to enslave other classes of workers in the coalmines—namely, the watermen, windsmen, and gatemen.

Able-bodied beggars could be pressed into service in the mines, and under the 1641 Act it was decreed that "because the said coal-hewers and salters and other workmen in the coal-heughs within this Kingdom do lie from their work at Pasch, Yule, Whit Sunday and certain other times in the year, which times they employ in drinking and debauchery, to the great offence of God and prejudice of their master, it is therefore Statute and ordained that the said coal-hewers and salters, and other workmen of coal-heughs in this Kingdom, work all the six days of the week . . ."

In defence of the masters, it can only be said that records of some pits in the Saltcoats district dating from the early part of the eighteenth century show that miners there were working a five-day week. Nonetheless, such humane employers were rare, and neither they nor the public at large, had a word to say about this shameful aspect of Scotland's industrial life. The miners were the lowest of the low, a class apart, and not deemed worthy even of the sympathy of their fellow men. They were better paid than many other workers, it is true, but they worked long hours underground—as many as fifteen or sixteen hours a day—and men were helped by their wives and children from generation to generation.

In 1775 an Act was passed to stop new enslavement and to allow for the eventual emancipation of those already in slavery after a period of time which depended on age and the availability of a replacement. It was 1799 before another Act declared all colliers in Scotland free men.

Writing much later, Lord Cockburn, who was a young Advocate at the time of the 1799 Act, said:

There are few people who now know that so recently as 1799 there were slaves in this country. Twenty-five years before, that is in 1775, there must have been thousands of them; for this was then the condition of all our colliers and salters. They were literally slaves. They could not be killed, nor directly tortured; but they belonged, like the serfs of an older time, to their respective works, with which they were sold as part of the gearing. With a few very rigid exceptions, the condition of the head of the family was the condition of the whole house. For though a child, *if never entered* with the work, was free, yet entering was its natural and almost certain destination, for its doing so was valuable to its father and its getting into any other employment in the neighbourhood was resisted by the owner. So that wives, daughters, and sons went on from generation to generation under a system which was the family doom. Of course, it was the interest of a wise master to use them well, as it was to use his other cattle well. But, as usual, the human animal had the worst of it. It had rights, and could provoke by alluding to them. It could alarm and mutiny. It could not be slain, but it had no protection against fits of tyranny or anger.

We do not know much of their exact personal or domestic condition. But we know what their work makes them, even when they are free, and within the jealous benevolence of a softer age. We know that they formed a separate and avoided tribe, as to a great extent they still do, with a language and habits of their own. And we know what slavery even in its best form is, and does.

The Acts which freed the miners caused no excitement—they were not even referred to in the *Scots Magazine* which commented on every aspect of Scottish life of the day. Although that last quarter of the eighteenth century was a time in which men cried out for liberty in many countries, no voice—not even that of Robert Burns, who was himself the evocation of equality and freedom—spared a moment to speak on behalf of the colliers. But then, as Lord Cockburn pointed out, the colliers were a separate and avoided tribe.

Having emancipated the miner the community did not accept him. He remained overworked and an outcast, so that he grew to be resentful of his master, opposed to the establishment, and a rebel against authority of any kind. In politics he is still a radical and bears the scars of the whipping that society has given him over three centuries. He lives in the midst of the farming community, but has little contact with it, except perhaps to poach an occasional rabbit. He has a fierce gambling instinct which leads him to play pitch and toss in his spare time, or to breed and train greyhounds or racing pigeons rather than to borrow books from the lending library. Although he is proud to see his son succeed (and many of them do) he often appears indifferent to learning. The mining community produces Keir Hardies rather than academics or scientists.

Perhaps the greatest change that has overtaken the mining community is the building of new housing to replace the drab lines of terraced room-and-kitchen cottages—the miners' 'raws'—of the villages near the coalpits. New townships have been built, and the houses in them are furnished lavishly and kept shining by

the womenfolk who themselves have grown up in the same community, and who are the hardest working and most intensely
houseproud women in Ayrshire. Their husbands should be proud
of them.

Because of the coal deposits, and the rich seams of iron which
also lay beneath Ayrshire, the northern half of the county became
highly industrialised during the nineteenth century. Fifty years
ago, Ayrshire was as important as Lanarkshire for ironsmelting,
but when it became cheaper to import ore than to mine it, the
county's iron industry declined until only one ironworks was left,
at Glengarnock.

The South-west has a great variety of industry, and this diversity
is the reason why the area has never suffered the devastating economic blight which has afflicted other parts of the country. Manufactures range from Johnnie Walker Whisky which has been
blended at Kilmarnock since grocer John Walker founded his
business in 1820, to the mining and manufacturing of hones,
which are used to whet sickles throughout the world. This rare
stone is found beside the river Ayr at Dalmore, near Stair—a part
of the river that Burns must have known well. Indeed, the industry originated during the poet's lifetime, in 1789, and it is carried
on by a company with the resounding name of The Water of Ayr
and Tam O' Shanter Hone Works Limited.

However, it is on engineering that the South-west's industrial
life has been based. And engineering skill has been turned to good
account in heavy engineering in Kilmarnock; die-stamping at
Ayr; and shipbuilding and repairing at Troon and Ayr. However,
these towns are not purely dependent on a single industry—
Kilmarnock also has light engineering, carpet-manufacturing,
shoe-making, textiles, and, of course, whisky. Ayr has much light
engineering, as well as chemical and carpet industries. To back the
heavy engineering there is light engineering—covering a multi-
tude of manufacturers throughout the northern half of the county,
and even outside the traditional industrial north as far south as
Girvan. Irvine and Kilwinning have their own industrial estates

offering factory space on the most advantageous terms to manufacturers, and other places like Cumnock and Maybole are making
a strong bid for industry, but with varying success. Maybole has
probably suffered harder than anywhere else in Ayrshire, for its
traditional agricultural engineering and footwear industries both
died away in the early 1960s. The town's plight was serious, and
early efforts to find new industry met with severe setbacks.
However, Maybole had survived the storms of centuries and its
council determined to survive this one. With foresight they
bought up sites and premises, and already they have attracted half
a dozen new firms into the town, providing five hundred new
jobs for the townspeople. These include packaging, printing,
clothing manufacture, fish processing and the making of motor
car silencers. Not a bad effort for a small country town! Not all of
the recently established engineering industry is either small or
light. The Kilmarnock area has been chosen by two internationally
famous companies for their new plant—Skefco, the Scandinavian
ball-bearing manufacturer, and Massey Harris, who make
combine harvesters here.

However, the engineering venture of which the South-west
should perhaps be proudest, is the one which has grown with
Prestwick International Airport in a great hangar which began life
as the Palace of Engineering at the 1938 Empire Exhibition in
Glasgow. Scottish Aviation has been many things in the years since
the Duke of Hamilton and the late Group Captain David McIntyre
founded the airfield before the Second World War. At first the
company developed Prestwick aerodrome and trained pilots.
Then during the war, when Prestwick became the busiest airfield
in the world, the company maintained, repaired and serviced
aeroplanes. It was against this background that Scottish Aviation
became involved in aircraft manufacture and light engineering.
For some time after the War the company, through its Scottish
Airlines division, operated a fleet of aircraft and pioneered many
routes to overseas destinations. The crippling effects of deliberate
restriction by the Government and the nationalisation of the air-

port, however, forced Scottish Aviation to withdraw these services and concentrate on its engineering projects. This led to the development of the Pioneer and Twin Pioneer series of aircraft, small planes which could land on a pocket handkerchief of land—a quality which made them highly suitable for civil operators in remote mountainous countries and for the Royal Air Force as well. These aircraft were produced in quantity until 1964, but manufacture has now ceased. Scottish Aviation are in 1972 producing in quantity the BULLDOG Basic Military Trainer of which over 200 are being produced for the Royal Air Force and the Armed Forces of Sweden, Kenya and Malaysia. The Company overhauls jet fighters for the Canadian Armed Forces in Europe and is a principal sub-contractor to Rolls-Royce for the production and overhaul of aero engine components and assemblies. In addition, airliners for the world's airlines are maintained and modified and the Company has also become a major supplier of fuselage panels for the Lockheed C.130 Hercules. At its Cumnock plant, Scottish Aviation has an advanced machining facility which is able to produce precision machined components for the Aerospace Industry and general engineering requirements. In an industry which has a high casualty rate, Scottish Aviation shows a remarkable ability to survive.

Engineering is important, but textiles are the traditional industry of Ayrshire. In Burns's time, the manufacture of stockings and bonnets was the stable industry of Ayrshire. The "guid blue bonnet" which Tam O' Shanter held fast as he "skelpit on" towards his rendezvous with the witches at Alloway was undoubtedly of local manufacture, originating in Kilmarnock most likely.

Stewarton was the centre of the stocking industry, but it was carried out in many villages right across the county boundary into Dumfriesshire. The First Statistical Account recorded that Sanquhar stockings had been exported to Virginia in large quantities until the Revolution had ruined the trade. They were so greatly admired that they had been worn by the Prince of Wales of the day.

Sanquhar gloves and stockings are knitted in black and white or in contrasting colours, in patterns which resemble the stitches of a sampler, and the owner's name can be worked round the leg or cuff. The patterns have names like The Duke's Pattern (the most popular one today), The Rose, and the Midge and Flea (which few people now know how to knit). Sanquhar knitting patterns almost died out, but they were rescued by a few people like Miss Ellen McGavin who acted to save them a generation ago.

"Over thirty years ago," wrote Miss McGavin, "there would only be three or four women in the town who could knit Sanquhar gloves, and it looked as if the pattern would die out. My mother and I went to an old lady whom we knew and she taught us. We went to her home every night until we had mastered it."

The gloves were knitted so that they could be worn on either hand, in order that the wearer could get maximum wear out of them—"A lesson in thrift, a thing almost forgotten in the present age," comments Miss McGavin.

The number of stitches never varies for any size of glove; the needles and wool are changed—thicker wool and needles for a large glove, and finer for a small one. Now the Sanquhar pattern is taught in schools in the town, so it should survive.

Commercially, textiles are still important to the South-west. In Ayrshire alone there are 120 firms employing ten thousand men and women to produce a great range of manufactures from cardigans to carpets, and blankets to Balmoral bonnets. Stewarton remains the commercial centre of the knitting industry, but knitwear is also manufactured in Kilmarnock and a number of other places, even as far away as Stranraer, where the firm of Cairnryan manufactures women's cardigans and sweaters.

When the handloom weaving died out, lace-making was introduced from Nottingham, and Ayrshire weavers took to the work so successfully that a thriving industry grew up to rival the city from which it was copied. Darvel and Newmilns in the upper —notably the disappearance of lace curtains—have hit it sorely. Catrine's cotton mill has gone, but they make man-made fibres at Dundonald. Tweeds, rugs and blankets are produced in a number of places, although the number of these is dwindling. My own home village of Minishant once had a blanket mill, which produced splendid blankets, but the industry is dead. Even Skeldon, whose blankets bear the legend 'Ye Banks and Braes O' Bonnie Doon', no longer manufactures, but is merely a store for blankets which have been woven elsewhere.

Special mention ought to be made of one thriving textile factory outside the industrial part of the South-west—at Newton Stewart in Wigtownshire. The Glen Cree Company has developed from a cotton mill powered by the waters of the river Cree two centuries ago, but which gave way to an ordinary grist mill for many years. During the last century the mill returned to textiles— to manufacture Galloway wool—the " 'oo' " of the rhyme:

> Kyle for a man,
> Carrick for a coo',
> Cunningham for butter and cheese,
> And Galloway for 'oo'.

They tell of a conversation between two Galloway worthies which went as follows:

"Is it 'oo'?"

"Aye."

"A' 'oo'?"

"Aye, a' 'oo'."

"A' ae 'oo'?"

"Aye, a' ae 'oo'."

"A' ae 'ear's 'oo'?"

"Aye, a' ae 'ear's 'oo'."

And if that needs translation, the final sentence means, "Yes, all one year's wool."

The Cree Woollen Mills manufactured much of Galloway's 'oo' for many years, but now it manufactures pure mohair blankets, rugs, stoles and scarves which are exported to fifty-four countries.

Perhaps the best known of the textile manufactures is the carpet industry which flourishes in both Ayr and Kilmarnock. Carpets have been made in Kilmarnock for more than two hundred years and from the first, this proved a most successful industry. By the early part of the nineteenth century it was the principal industry of the town. The New Statistical Account reported: "In carpet factories about 1,200 people are employed in weaving Brussels, Venetian, Turkey and Scotch carpets and rugs, the quality and patterns of which are not surpassed by any in Britain. The annual value of this branch of trade is about £150,000." One hundred and fifty thousand pounds in 1842—that was a sizeable industry, and a great many companies participated in it. Today, there is only one—Blackwood, Morton and Sons Limited, whose trademark, of a gambolling lamb with the letters "BMK" is worldwide. The rise of the company in this century has been phenomenal—in the decade leading up to 1939 output increased by 1,000 per cent, and in 1939 there were 1,800 workers in the factory producing *each week* 5,000 carpets, 12,000 rugs and 20,000 yards of piece goods. Post-war progress has been similarly impressive, and output now stands at some £10 million per annum.

Ayr's carpet-manufacturing company dates from 1876 when William C. Gray bought two handlooms and set two weavers to work making carpets in the town. Within a year he had transferred his business to larger premises across the river in Newton-on-Ayr, and had a dozen weavers at his looms. Gray's 'Twelve Apostles', as his workmen were known, soon multiplied into a small army of weavers who had brought to Ayr a great industry. William C. Gray and Sons is now part of a carpet empire which stretches halfway round the world, and when a subsidiary company was formed in Tasmania in 1961 to manufacture Axminster carpets for the Australian market, the labour force was recruited in Ayr. Gray's of Ayr have introduced many exotic and colourful designs in recent years, ranging from impressionist patterns to genuine tartans. The most unusual, however, is the Burns Rug, which bears a portrait of the poet surrounded by four scenes—the

Cottage at Alloway, Alloway Auld Kirk, Burns Monument at Alloway, and the Tam O' Shanter Inn at Ayr. All this is contained in a border of Wallace tartan to commemorate Sir William Wallace's association with Ayr. The Burns Rug is woven in thirty-seven shades, and it has found a ready market among Burns enthusiasts throughout the world. Attractive as the rug may be, it does seem wrong to wipe one's feet on the Bard's face. Burns would have had a comment on it, no doubt, in verse!

Technically outside the Burns Country, but of much influence within it, is the great Imperial Chemical Industries factories complex at Stevenston. In addition to explosives manufacture, originally established at Ardeer by Alfred Nobel in 1871, the company has an extensive manufacture of chemical products; nitric and sulphuric acids; cellulose products; silicones; chemicals for the coating, foodstuffs, transparent paper, adhesives, paints and varnish industry; 'nylon salt' (an intermediate in the manufacture of nylon); and Melinex and Propathane, forms of transparent polyester film used for packaging, especially in the foodstuffs industry. These products are manufactured in three factories at Stevenston and two at Dumfries.

The Alginates Industries factory at Girvan turns Hebridean seaweed into a large variety of products, including custard powder. William Grant and Sons have also established a whisky distillery within the confines of a former explosives factory at Girvan.

The other major industry in Dumfries is a new one, but it is housed in a factory where the pioneer Arrol Johnston motor cars were manufactured more than half a century ago. When the North British Rubber Company outgrew its home at Castle Mills in Edinburgh, it chose as the site for its overflow factory the disused Arrol Johnston works at Heathhall, Dumfries.

The new branch of the company, started in 1946, now turns out rubber and plastic products—footwear, conveyor belting, carpet underlay, golf balls, and more than half of the bathing caps that are manufactured in Britain. Progress has brought further expansion and the North British is now part of the vast United States Rubber Company, whose name, UniRoyal, it has now adopted.

Galloway is untouched by the black fingers of industry. Glen Cree rugs, Cairnryan knitwear, Ladybird children's clothes and Baby Deer children's shoes at Stranraer hardly amount to industrialisation, although the province is anxious to attract companies which want more scope than can be found south of the English Border or in the Central Plain of Scotland. The story of Galloway's industry is that of processing her natural resources and the produce of the land. Creameries, agricultural implement repairers, cattle transporters, and the like employ more men than factories do. The granite of Dalbeattie and Creetown form the basis of a thriving industry, although the stone is now too expensive to be used much for houses, public buildings and public works such as the breakwater at Port of Spain in Trinidad. Instead, it is used for road works nearer home.

Yet Galloway might have been a great centre of industry—one hesitates in the light of past experience to say *might yet be* an important manufacturing and trading centre. The story is one of despoiling by the shore of Loch Ryan, where the village of Cairnryan stood on the main road from Stranraer to Glasgow, a pleasant little unimportant and unspoilt place, until the Second World War came and the Government decided to build a deep-water harbour for use in case Glasgow and Liverpool were bombed. The channel at the mouth of the loch was widened to 500 feet and a 2,400 foot long deep-water jetty was built capable of taking ships of a draught of up to 30 feet. A second wharf was built for small vessels, and railway marshalling yards extending to twenty miles of track were laid out. By the lochside stood a row of great cranes, crouched over the grey water like giant anglers waiting for a nibble on the end of their line, and to complete the work a tall fence enclosed the whole port.

Cairnryan gave good service during the war. Churchill sailed from it, and so did the King and Queen on their way to Canada.

Captured German U-boats were coralled there, and parts of the mulberry harbour, which facilitated the invasion of Europe in 1944, were built there. Even when hostilities ended, Cairnryan remained busy as a centre for breaking up warships. But in time, this work diminished and the port itself began to crumble. It was clear that the Government had lost interest in the harbour and in the men whose livelihood depended on it. By 1959, 370 men were rendered idle and the War Department had stripped the port of everything that could be taken away, and Cairnryan was sold off to a Portsmouth scrap merchant for £250,000, a fraction of what it had cost. There were supposed to be guarantees that Cairnryan would be revived and provide much needed work for local men. As *The Scotsman* described it in 1965: "It became the white hope of Scotland's South-west; but it was to become its white elephant. During the war, in time of crisis, money was poured into it; but for the last seven years it has been a pawn in the hands of London financiers speculating for quick profit."

On several occasions, hopes rose that Cairnryan would be revived, but every time the plan proved abortive. Today the harbour stands derelict and Cairnryan village is still separated from the loch by the old railways. The only hope—and it would be a hope for the far, far future—might be the building of the much talked of barrage across the Solway to turn the South-west corner of Scotland into a vast industrial centre, with Cairnryan as its seaport. But by that time, the last of the jetties and wharves will have toppled into the loch, and it will be easier to start from scratch and despoil another village.

X

EVEN AFRICAN CHIEFS DANCE

THE working life of people in our part of the world may have lost some of that harshness that characterised it half a century ago, and certainly I never hear people boast of the feats which my father tells of. There were no cars when he was young, and it was nothing to walk one's cattle miles to market and then to herd them home again if the price offered did not please.

If work is less rigorous, play is not. The noise which emanates from any village hall on the evening of a dance suggests that we know how to make the fullest use of our leisure—blood-curdling whoops that would have turned Redskins pale drown the music throughout the dancing of an eightsome reel until a triumphant yell of "Best set in the hall" ends it. To participate requires about as much energy as shepherding a dozen flighty hens across a busy road, and as the majority of the dancers are farmers they are well practised in such things.

It can be dangerous even to watch, for the dance sweeps to and fro like a miniature Calgary stampede and only the fleet of foot can escape. The simple act of turning one's partner is a full-blooded Scottish 'birl' in which the girl (and at times her partner also) leave the floor or slide along the polished surface like curling stones until their progress is halted by a wall or some other couple hurtling in the opposite direction.

No one who witnesses this would say that Scotsmen lack a

capacity for enjoyment—and yet, we do tend to take our pleasures seriously. I do not mean that we do not know how to enjoy ourselves, but that we have something of a guilt complex about recreation that makes us immerse ourselves in it.

Dances take place in the hall, so of course this is the centre of social life in the community. The hall is often named after some eminent benefactor to the community (usually one of the landed families in the neighbourhood) so its name is often so splendid-sounding that the actual hall cannot match up to it. How, for example, could any hall live up to a name like the Claude Hamilton Memorial Hall? Of late names have tended to run to Community Centre instead of village hall, and that is a fair description of the place's function.

Whatever its name may be—hall or community centre—this is the hub of the district's recreation. Here they play badminton and carpet bowls, whist and bingo. Here members of the Scottish Women's Rural Institute gather to test their strawberry jam against that of their neighbours. And here the old and the young gather for their Christmas treats.

One learns the harshness of life at such functions; I once cried all the way home from the Sunday School Christmas Party because no one had chosen me for a partner at 'Bee, Baw, Babbity', our Kissing-in-the-Ring game. Round and round I had gone singing

> Bee, Baw, Babbity,
> Bee, Baw, Babbity,
> Bee, Baw, Babbity,
> Kiss a bonnie wee laddie.
> I widnae hae a laddie-o,
> A laddie-o, a laddie-o.
> I widnae hae a laddie-o.
> I'd rather hae a wee lassie.

When the music stopped I waited to be chosen and kissed, but it never happened, and I went home disillusioned and disappointed.

Apart from the shop, the hall is the chief centre of news in any district. Here information is received and passed on, crops are discussed, bargains are struck, reputations are made and lost, and feuds are begun but seldom ended. The hall may be a happy place, but it is a dangerous place also, for gossip always brings trouble.

During the last two generations women have come to be a greater force in the community's recreational life. For one thing they are better organised, and for another they are needed to prepare food and refreshments and to serve these at every function. The men may join the management committee, but that is as far as they go—the work is strictly for the womenfolk.

The chief reason for the women's superiority is the 'Rural', the Scottish Women's Rural Institute. The 'Rural' grew out of the First World War when the role of woman in the community began to change, and the spread of the movement has been spectacular. In the Stewartry of Kircudbright, for example, the first institute was formed at Twynholm in 1920, and by 1924 the number had grown to twenty-three. Now there are more than fifty institutes in the Stewartry alone. The 'Rural' is an essential part of the countrywoman's life, just as the Townswomen's Guild is the focus of life in the towns. It has, of course, a strong practical bias, organising competitions and demonstrations of cookery and crafts, but its work extends much further—the 'Rural' does much charitable work, and it is an important pillar of most of the agricultural shows in the country. Without the baking and crafts classes many of these shows would be poor affairs.

The women will tackle anything. My mother's institute once acted as hosts to a dozen African tribal chiefs, plying them with home-baked scones and pancakes and initiating them into the ritual of Scottish country dancing. The chiefs were startled at first, but they allowed themselves to be pushed through the figures of the dances, and they must have gone home of the firm opinion that Scottish society is a strongly matriarchal one.

Dundrennan Abbey—sad beauty enfolded in the hills
Crossraguel Abbey—archways defy time

Agricultural shows are not what they once were in the South-west. A generation ago every village had its own show which was keenly contested by local farmers and not, as so many now are, a great advertising spree for food and machinery manufacturers and a showplace for a few big farmers. Rising costs killed the smaller shows, and, while one must acknowledge the place for progress in farming life, one must regret the fact that smaller farmers who readily competed in their own district are now frightened away from the bigger shows.

However, there is one important show that is new to the region—Ayr's annual flower show, which has risen in the space of a decade to a display of national importance, with some five thousand entries from every part of the country each year. Again, this success (in part at least) is due to the influence of the women, for their handicrafts and baking sections make a major contribution to it.

The men come into their own in sport, and here there is a distinct cleavage between the townsman whose main interests are bowls and golf, and the countryman who veers towards field sports and curling. Country and town are linked, however, in Scotland's most popular game (one is tempted to say craze)—football. Fitba' daft! That epithet applies to almost anywhere in Scotland, and it is certainly true of the South-western corner.

Hats—or more appropriately—bonnets are raised to Kilmarnock, the most successful professional soccer team in South-west Scotland in recent years. 'Killie' were Scottish League champions in season 1964–65, but their fortunes have waned somewhat in recent years, when they have not succeeded in maintaining a position in the top half of the league table. This has brought a fall in support to less than five thousand for home games, for fans in the world of football are as fickle as those in any other sport. As a result the club has lost good players, and has turned from full-time to part-time football. And even then it has difficulty in making its books balance.

The honest men of Ayr United have fared better. After topping

Football and bowls at Dalmellington
"Walking the dogs" at Dalbeattie

the Second Division table in 1959 they were demoted and promoted annually from one division to another, and support fell away. At last they have settled down as a good team—good enough to reach the semi-final of the Scottish League Cup, and their supporters have returned. Thus the Honest Men, who were in serious danger of disappearing a decade ago, are back in business. Their club even made a profit in 1971!

The third major team in the South-west is Queen of the South—the 'Doonhamers' as they are nicknamed—from Dumfries. They have a good ground and a fair following, but they seem unable to find their way back to the top division where they once were.

The bigger teams have their following, but soccer in these parts is not merely a spectator sport. Nor is it just a winter one. On Saturday afternoons and on most weekday evenings village youths gather to kick a ball around, either as an organised team or just for fun. They train and practise assiduously, many of them dreaming of the time when they may be chosen to play professionally, and on weekend afternoons parks are packed with teams taking part in league matches—from under eleven-year-olds to seniors. And Ayr even has a flourishing pub league!

In the mining villages football is followed in popularity by greyhound racing, pigeon racing and bowling. The miners have a strongly competitive streak in their make-up, and day after day they spend all their leisure time walking the dogs in preparation for racing at the stadium at Ayr, or at smaller meetings which are held in open fields.

Blood sports—foxhunting, otter-hunting, grouse shooting and hare coursing—all continue in various places, particularly among the landowners and the farmers, although the farmer's interest tends to be to reduce vermin or to bag a rabbit or a brace of pigeons for the pot. The most unusual of these sports is otter-hunting, which has been popular on the riverbanks of both Ayrshire and Dumfriesshire for many years. Even the Artillery Regiment stationed at Dundonald Camp used to keep its own pack of otter hounds and hunt the rivers of central Ayrshire twice a week until the regiment was mobilised at the time of the Suez crisis, and the pack had to be disbanded.

The farmers take some interest in blood sports, but the pastime which they have made their own is the roaring game—curling. This is appropriate, for Ayrshire is the home of the manufacture of curling stones. It is now two centuries since Burns satirised Tam Samson and his friends who hastened to the frozen loch 'wi' gleesome speed' to curl, and Tam was stationed at the cock

> To guard, or draw, or wick a bore,
> Or up the rink like Jehu roar
> In time o' need.

Nowadays farmers do not have to wait for winter to muffle up its cloak; they enjoy the roaring game on artificial ice at ice rinks all the year round. From Dumfriesshire, Kirkcudbright. and Wigtownshire they come 'wi gleesome speed' to attend the Tuesday market in Ayr or the Thursday sheep sales, and afterwards to retire to a game of curling. Times do not change; they still roar up the rink like Jehu, sweeping the ice before the running stones and crying, 'Soop, man, soop. For God's sake soop.' The curlers have their own songs and matches which have become traditional in the district.

The townsman sometimes joins the countryman in his pastimes, but the game which he has made his own is golf. There is no better golfing country in the whole of Scotland than Ayrshire, where the smallest town has at least nine modest holes, and the bigger places have two or more courses. The great golfing towns are Prestwick, which has two famous courses, and Troon which has five courses around it.

The greatest of the Troon golf links is the Old Course, which has been the venue of many epic golfing battles including the Open and Amateur Championships. The Old Course runs along the edge of the Firth of Clyde and, like so many of the Ayrshire courses, may be enjoyed for its scenery as much as for the sport that it affords. It is a testing course, the names of the holes—

Turnberry, Ailsa, the Railway, Tel-el-Kebir and Sandhills—mean different memories to different golfers, for every player has his tale of triumph and disaster on each and every one.

The Portland Course is the home of Troon Ladies' Club, but that does not mean that it is an easy course. Indeed, qualifying rounds of the Open have been played here. Local people call the Lochgreen Course the best walk in Ayrshire because it has a number of long holes which call for hard hitting, and the Darley Course has a burn running through which has to be crossed six times. The last of the Troon Courses is the Fullarton, the easiest of the five, but still worth playing.

Troon's golf courses are not merely for the enjoyment of local folk. The South-west of Scotland is a recreational centre for the whole of Scotland and for many visitors from England and over-seas as well. Of course it has an advantage over many other parts for one Canadian in three who visits Britain arrives at Prestwick and one American in four arrives there. As a result the pattern of holidaymaking has changed in recent years. The main coastal towns with their gently-sloping beaches were once filled almost exclusively with Glaswegians who came lock, stock and cabin trunk for a month 'doon the watter'. Now the Ayrshire coast is a short motor journey away from Glasgow so they can come on any sunny day and return home the same evening. In fact large numbers come in hired coaches, and the wilder elements of these have caused such disturbance that they are forced to leave before a certain time and it is made clear that they will not be welcome any later.

As a result of the changing pattern of holidaymaking, Ayrshire has suffered a decline in the number of overnight visitors to her resorts. A survey a few years ago put the annual loss at 80,000 visitors, but tourism has now become one of the country's most important industries.

Inland, tourism has been badly neglected also—the places with which Robert Burns was connected have been allowed to be modernised out of recognition and signposts are so few that they are hard to find by the visitor who has paid us the compliment of travelling as much as half way round the world to see them. The shining exception in the whole of the Burns Country (outside Alloway, which *is* Burns) is Ellisland. Here one may stand in the neatly-kept farmyard and feel that this is the real Burns Country as Burns knew it. And discreet notices indicate points of interest where the Bard wrote his poems.

The coastal villages and the empty hills of Galloway have only recently begun to be discovered by holidaymakers from other parts of Scotland and especially from the North of England. Lancastrians, finding the Lake District crowded and spoilt, have discovered that in little more than an hour they can drive through Dumfries into Glen Trool Forest Park where there are superb hill walks, great fishing, and beautiful empty landscapes waiting for them. On the coast the little harbours of Kippford, Rockcliffe and the Isle of Whithorn are developing as yachting centres to such a degree that I recently saw this coast described as the Riviera of Scotland!

The inhabitants of the South-west in general welcome the increase in tourism for this provides them with much needed extra income. Indeed, bed and breakfast signs are so numerous at farm road-ends that one wonders if this is the new 'perk' of the farmer's wife in place of the proceeds of the henruns from which she once dressed herself and provided luxuries for her family. Those who derive no direct financial benefit from tourism may be a little less welcoming to the new trend, for they see it as a threat to their beautiful little world.

Nonetheless, the process has begun, and it cannot be stopped. There is still room for many, many more tourists without spoiling the natural beauty of the area. One hopes that the process will continue, but that it will never pass the point where the area is ruined for those who live in it.

XI

MARKS OF MAN

NATURE has been generous to the Burns Country; man has been
less so. And yet, when one considers the damage that has been
done to beautiful countryside elsewhere, we in the Burns Country
are fortunate.

Roads of the South-west are good, which is as they should be
in the native country of John Loudon Macadam, the man who
devised a new method of highway construction and added a word
to the English language—macadamise. Macadam was born at
Ayr, and he experimented with his roadbuilding method at
Sauchrie, his home on the slope of the Carrick hills near Ayr.
Although much of his important road-building was done in
England, they still point out a piece of road at Sauchrie which was
the first macadamised road in the country.

There was plenty of scope for Macadam's work, for roads had
been poor hitherto. As long ago as the sixteenth century King
James was so buffeted on a journey through Ayrshire that he
threatened to send the next man against whom he bore a grudge
to attend a wedding at Sorn. Burns, too, complained bitterly
about Ayrshire highways, and wrote an epigram about the one
between Kilmarnock and Stewarton.

> I'm now arrived, thanks to the gods!
> Thro' pathways rough and muddy—
> A certain sign that making roads

Is not this people's study.
And tho' I'm not with scripture crammed,
I'm sure the bible says
That heedless sinners shall be damned
Unless they mend their ways.

Even at the end of Burns's lifetime, the First Statistical Account reported that until recently most roads "through the shire of Air" were barely passable. However, Macadam and his work were soon to alter that.

Over the past century a network of good roads has been constructed throughout the South-west, and, although there is not a mile of motorway in the region yet, some new highway has been constructed, mainly to bypass the bigger towns. One of the most remarkable results of these roadmaking operations has been the new vistas that they have opened up. One drives along the Ayr bypass and looks across a scene which Burns must have known well as he rode into the town from Tarbolton. The other major change in roads is the ironing out of bends that has taken place especially among the hills of Galloway. The roads no longer twist across the moors, but stride decisively towards the next village, and the oxbow loops which have been bypassed are used as parking and picnicking places for travellers.

Of course, the motor-car has revolutionised transport in the South-west as it has done everywhere, but the region still has a wonderful network of bus services. After half a century in which small operators were squeezed out or swallowed up by larger units, the main transport service is operated by the state-owned Western Scottish Motor Traction Company, and when one experiences bus services elsewhere in Britain, one is thankful for the large numbers of buses on the roads of the Burns Country. A few smaller companies endure despite the domination of the Western S.M.T., notably an unusual association of companies such as A1 and AA whose southern limit is Ayr.

Roads were pioneered in Ayrshire; so were railways. A line was built and horsedrawn trains ran between Kilmarnock and Troon

as early as 1812, and when steam power arrived a line was opened
between Ayr and Irvine in 1839. Within a year, Ayr was linked to
Glasgow by railway, and then eyes began to look towards the
South and the rich trade across the Border. Eventually, the lines in
the South-west belonged to two companies, the Glasgow and
South Western Railway and the Caledonian Railway whose lines
formed a great triangle with Glasgow as its topmost apex and a
railway from Dumfries to Stranraer as its base. From this triangle
ran many small lines to Turnberry, Dalmellington, Mauchline,
Portpatrick, Whithorn, Kirkcudbright and Moniaive, but these
were gradually whittled away over the years, and now a whole
side of the triangle—from Dumfries to Stranraer—has been lopped
off, leaving little of the original network. The future of the rem-
nant that is left is far from secure.

Of course, progress which has destroyed the railways has
brought air travel, and Ayrshire is Scotland's air crossroads. Prestwick was built by the late Group Captain David MacIntyre and
the Duke of Hamilton, and after proving its value in the war, it
was threatened with closure on a number of occasions. But the
fact remains that Prestwick is freer from fog than most other air-
ports, and that is a strong reason for retaining it. Now it looks as if
Prestwick's future is safe, for a great glass-walled terminal has been
built to handle the traffic. Here travellers from North America
and Europe pass through a tartan corridor into Scotland.

BUILDINGS IN THE SOUTH-WEST

One finds little planning and almost no distinguished architecture in the South-west, although the whole effect adds up to a feeling of warm friendliness. The reason is that for many generations
the principal building material was red sandstone, whose colour is
a glowing reddish brown, which mellows with time to turn the
most ordinary architecture into something attractive.

The building stone is the best feature of most of the buildings in
the region for, unfortunately, there is no long tradition of great

and noble houses. While the English aristocracy were founding the first stately homes, Scotland was still rent by feuds and wars in which the first action of any side was to destroy his enemy's houses. As a result, the homes of the Kennedys, Crawfords and Campbells were not noble castles but four-square fortresses with the minimum of windows and doors. Some of these castles are still inhabited, although in many cases so many alterations and additions have been made that the original building can barely be discerned. The vast majority, however, lie in ruins, often close to a modern mansion bearing the same name.

The many castles running all the way from Dundonald Castle in Kyle to Caerlaverock, south-east of Dumfries, testify to the number and strength of these fortresses—the walls of Loch Doon Castle are between seven and nine feet thick in places, and Cassillis House has sixteen-foot walls at its base. In these castles kings held court, kings were born, and kings died. Robert the Bruce's birthplace was Turnberry Castle, the first of the Stuart kings, Robert II, died at Dundonald, and Mary Stuart is said to have stayed at Newark after the Battle of Longside.

The Ministry of Public Building and Works has taken many of these castles into its care and stopped the process of decay. Among those which now belong to the Ministry are Dundonald and Loch Doon in Ayrshire; the Castle of Park at Glenluce, Wigtownshire; Caerlaverock and Lochmaben in Dumfriesshire; and a number in the Stewartry of Kirkcudbright—the McCulloch stronghold of Cardoness, Carsluith, Maclellan's Castle, the unique fifteenth-century round tower of Orchardton, and Threave Castle which Archibald the Grim, third Earl of Douglas, built in the fourteenth century.

A number of ancient houses are still inhabited. Cassillis and Killochan have changed little in four centuries, apart from having central heating and modern amenities added. However, the majority of the ancient houses have been rebuilt on other sites. The Black Douglas castle at Threave lies in ruins, but Threave House, which was built in 1870, now belongs to the National

Trust for Scotland and is run as a school of gardening to fill the gap in the training of young gardeners that was left by the decline of the great private gardens.

As it lies within easy reach of the industrial part of Scotland the South-west has many fine houses built as country seats for successful manufacturers in the last century. However, the two greatest houses of the area are much longer established than that. Drumlanrig Castle lies in Nithsdale, just north of Thornhill and, although it is not open to the public, one can catch glimpses of its turreted magnificence from the road. Drumlanrig is the home of the Duke of Buccleuch, whose ancestor the first Earl of Queensberry built the castle between 1679 and 1689. Ironically, the ill-tempered earl who built Drumlanrig spent only one night under its roof.

Culzean Castle, pronounced *Cullane* to rhyme with *pain*, is the most famous of all the great houses in the Burns Country; indeed, royal homes and Edinburgh Castle apart, it is the best-known castle in the whole of Scotland. The grounds of Culzean have been developed as Scotland's first country park, run by three local authorities.

Culzean stands on a clifftop on the coast between Ayr and Girvan, a piece of Georgian glory set in gardens of great beauty and sub-tropical lushness. When the Earl of Cassillis decided to rebuild the ancient castle about the middle of the eighteenth century he chose as his architect Robert Adam, the greatest architectural genius Scotland has ever produced. Adam's work has been preserved by the National Trust for Scotland who now own Culzean, and even the original moulds, which had lain in the workshop of a Maybole tradesman for a hundred and fifty years, were used to preserve its Georgian splendour. The castle is now open to the public and it is one of the Trust's most popular showplaces; 100,000 people come to Culzean each year to admire the gracious exterior, the elegant oval staircase, the armoury and—best of all— the superb round drawing room, whose windows overlook the Firth of Clyde two hundred feet below.

When Culzean Castle was taken over by the National Trust for Scotland its top floor was converted into a kind of grace and favour flat to be put at the disposal of someone whom the Scottish people wished to honour. The choice of first tenant fell upon General Dwight D. Eisenhower, later President of the United States of America, in recognition of his services during the Second World War. As a keen golfer, General Eisenhower enjoyed a number of visits to his home in the heart of some of Scotland's finest golfing country.

For a time after he presented the castle to the National Trust for Scotland, the Marquis of Ailsa continued to live in a wing which had been added to Adam's design in the last century, but he moved to another ancient Kennedy stronghold—Cassillis House— and the nineteenth-century wing at Culzean was converted into three flats for letting by the National Trust.

The lack of fine castles in South-west Scotland is more than compensated for by the glory of medieval ecclesiastical architecture. The story of the abbeys has already been told, so it is sufficient to refer to the rich stonework of Sweetheart, the lofty sadness of Dundrennan and the neat utility of layout at Crossraguel. Even after four centuries of depredations by weather and post-Reformation house-builders the abbeys stand in magnificence.

Apart from the abbeys few pre-Reformation churches survive. One can still see the bare shell of St. Ninian's Chapel at the Isle of Whithorn, the Collegiate Church of Maybole, and gaunt walls of Kirkoswald, St. Nicholas's Kirk at Prestwick, and Alloway Auld Kirk, but none of them is particularly attractive. To compensate, we have a few early post-Reformation churches like Ayr's Auld Kirk, which was built in 1655, and which is a beautiful, severe cruciform building set behind the town's High Street, out of sight and sound of the daily life of the town.

In the villages one also finds an occasional church to admire, but on the whole, the kirks of the South-west are interesting rather than fine specimens of architecture. The reasons are threefold; in the first place, the Presbyterian religion does not

encourage ostentation or embellishment; secondly, the fabric of
the churches was for many years in the care of heritors, who were
canny folk, not given to spending money needlessly; and thirdly,
schisms divided the kirk to such a degree that the smallest villages
had two or even three rival kirks. After the Great Disruption of
1843, the seceders needed places of worship urgently, and there
was neither time nor money to produce beautiful buildings. As a
result, Scotland is the poorer architecturally.

THE FARMS

By preserving the cottage where Burns was born, and other
buildings associated with him, we have been given a glimpse of
the way in which our great-grandfathers lived. And when one
views the but-and-ben at Alloway with the byre and barn leading
straight out of it, one realises that farmers have come a long way
in two centuries. Indeed, the majority of farmhouses have been
rebuilt since 1800. The New Statistical Account for Dalrymple
reported that about half of the farmhouses and steadings in the
parish had been rebuilt between 1800 and 1837.

For many years farmsteads were built to a pattern—barns,
house and byre enclosed a yard which was called 'the close', and
somewhere at the back was set a large red-painted iron shed to
store hay. The rough stone walls of the buildings were whitewashed and the lintels of doors and windows were painted red.
Now more colourful washes are beginning to be used and the red
haysheds are being replaced by giant silos and grain stores.

Social upheavals, which have prevented farmers from setting
their sons up in farms, have led to another change; often a bungalow has been built at the end of the farm road to house the retiring
parents as the next generation takes over.

If farms have improved so, too, have villages and towns. For
many years, largely due to the war, there was an air of decay and
neglect throughout Scotland. In my own village of Minishant a
group of handsome timber houses was built just before the war

and people from the straggling row of room-and-kitchen cottages which came to be known as 'the old village' were moved into this 'new village'. The empty houses decayed and a few were demolished before war came and evacuee families from Glasgow moved into those which remained. Of course, the end of the war brought an urgent need for homes and the old houses are not only still occupied, but look better than they have ever done. Interiors have been modernised and exteriors painted so that houses which stood desolate and decaying thirty years ago are attractive cottages. And the village is much the better for the change.

ALLOWAY

In describing what man has built—and destroyed—in the Burns Country, one must start at Alloway. Centuries ago Alloway was important only because the high, hump-backed arch there was the only bridge to span the Doon. However, the birth of Robert Burns made Alloway the most celebrated village in Scotland. Alloway carries its fame modestly—it remains an unpretentious place, a rather well-bred suburb of Ayr, with fine houses half hidden behind high walls, the town's cricket ground, the town's only boys' preparatory school, and Belleisle gardens and golf course nearby. Alloway folk lead normal lives, running kirk sales of work and whist drives, but to the world at large, Alloway is a very special place.

The cottage where the poet was born looks almost exactly as it did two hundred years ago, although its immediate surroundings have changed. When William Burnes moved to Mount Oliphant, he continued to own the cottage until 1781 when it was sold to the Incorporation of Shoemakers in Ayr, and for the next century it was a public house. In 1881 the trustees of Burns's Monument bought the cottage and restored it to its original appearance. A museum has been added and the trustees have attempted to purchase every major relic of the poet that has come on the market.

The cottage stands apart from the other Alloway links with

Burns. A mile along the road, and out of sight, lie the Auld Kirk, the Bridge of Doon, and Burns Monument. First comes the church, set above the road and so enveloped in trees that even on a summer's day it feels remote from the world around it. On a winter's night, it is a ghostly place. The Auld Kirk of Alloway was a ruin even in Burns's day, but farmers and merchants continued to be interred in its graveyard for a century afterwards. Here lie Burns's father and my own great-grandparents; the epitaph to William Burnes speaking for them and for all other farmers and merchants who are buried there:

> O ye whose cheek the tear of pity stains,
> Draw near with pious rev'rence, and attend!
> Here lie the loving husband's dear remains,
> The tender father, and the gen'rous friend.
> The pitying heart that felt for human woe;
> The dauntless heart that fear'd no human pride
> The friend of man, to vice alone a foe;
> For 'ev'n his failings lean'd to virtue's side'.

But what would William Burnes and his fellows think had they known that their resting place would be better known for an imaginery dance of witches. It all began when a Carrick farmer, Tam O' Shanter, spent too convivial an evening in Ayr, and then rode home by the old road which ran from Ayr to Alloway— closer to the coast than the present one and curving behind the Auld Kirk to the Brig' O' Doon. As Tam reached the church, he found it "in a bleeze" of light with witches and warlocks dancing furiously under the eye of Old Nick himself. As Tam watched the dancing became faster and more furious:

> They reel'd, they set, they cross'd, they cleekit[1]
> Till ilka carlin swat and reekit,
> And coost her duddies[2] to the wark
> And linkit at it in her sark[3].

[1] linked arms.
[2] cast her clothes.
[3] shirt.

The dancers were outclassed by one named Nannie, who wore a skirt so short that Tam forgot himself and cried out, 'Weel done Cutty sark[1]'. In an instant the kirk was plunged into darkness and the 'hellish legion' streamed out after Tam and his mare Meg, who were already rushing for the safety of the bridge. Nannie led the chase. . . .

> . . . far before the rest,
> Hard upon noble Maggie prest,
> And flew at Tam wi' furious ettle;
> But little wist[2] she Maggie's mettle!
> Ae spring brought off her master hale[3],
> But left behind her ain grey tail;
> The carlin caught her by the rump,
> And left poor Maggie scarce a stump.

Within a generation of the death of Burns, Alexander Boswell, son of Dr. Johnson's biographer, instigated a plan to erect a memorial at Alloway. A meeting was duly convened and carefully reported—On the motion of the Rev. Hamilton Paul, Boswell was called to the chair, and on the chairman's motion Paul was appointed secretary. Again on a motion from the chair, seconded by the secretary, it was agreed that steps be taken to erect a monument to the bard. The secretary then proposed, and the chairman seconded a motion that Boswell be elected convener and Paul be elected secretary of the movement. A vote of thanks to the chairman proposed by the secretary, concluded the business, and the meeting scaled. In fact, only two people—Boswell and Paul—had been present!

Although support was poor initially, Scotsmen soon rallied to subscribe £3,000 to build the monument which now stands on the hill above the old Brig' O' Doon at Alloway. Nine graceful Corinthian pillars, one for each of the muses, are crowned by a

[1] short skirt.
[2] knew.
[3] whole.

cupola, and the base houses a small collection of Burns relics—among them Jean Armour's wedding ring, the Bible which Burns gave to Highland Mary, and a pair of drinking glasses which he gave to Clarinda. Surely as tasteless a juxtaposition of Burnsiana as one is likely to find anywhere.

Ayr

Alloway is now a suburb of Ayr, for the county town has sprawled south beyond the River Doon, north to meet Prestwick, and eastwards into Kyle. Ayr is a charming town, with the dignity that befits a place with a long pedigree. They will tell you in Ayr that they do not know when the town was founded, but that it was important enough to be elevated to the status of a royal burgh in 1202. Its castle was fought over during the defence of Scotland, and after freedom was won King Robert the Bruce called his Parliament at Ayr to establish the succession through the heirs of his daughter Marjorie—the beginning of the long and unhappy line of Stewarts.

Despite this history, Ayr is not an old town architecturally. There is scarcely a fragment left even of the town of Burns's time —the castle has been completely destroyed, only a tall square tower remains of the pre-Reformation church of St. John the Baptist, and Loudon Hall, the oldest building standing in the town, dates back only four centuries. Of course, one can still walk across the steeply arched medieval bridge which is said to have been put up by two sisters as a memorial to their lovers who were drowned while trying to ford the flooded River Ayr to visit them. The Auld Brig had a narrow escape at the beginning of the present century when it fell into such disrepair that it threatened to emulate the "conceited gowk" of a New Bridge downriver from it and collapse. However, the bridge was saved, and it still serves as a pedestrian way from Ayr to Newton-on-Ayr.

Of the thatched houses that filled the town in Burns's day only the Tam O' Shanter Inn, where Tam spent that merry evening

Miss Ellen McGavin knits Sanquhar pattern
Mr. Thomas Lochhead works at his potter's wheel in
Kirkcudbright

before he encountered the witches, remains. The inn is no longer a public house, but has been turned into yet another museum of Burns Country relics. A few of the old wynds exist in name, but their appearance has changed greatly in recent years. They are no longer narrow, rough alleyways lined with but-and-ben cottages, but have trim shops and offices along them. The Fish and Malt Crosses, the Mealmarket and the town jail have gone also—the last an improvement if one is to judge by the comment of *The Edinburgh Encyclopaedia* which described the jail as "not so much the terror of evildoers as the horror of those who do well." In place of the "Auld Toure", Ayr has a fussy Victorian Gothic Wallace Tower which offends nearly as many eyes today as the jail did two hundred years ago. The Wallace Tower chokes the High Street and from time to time it is threatened with demolition to speed the flow of traffic.

Ayr has some elegant townplanning especially around Wellington Square, where the County Buildings overlook gardens on one side and the sea on the other. However, the spacious streets of villas built in the past century have been marred by a suburban sprawl of characterless boxes which are graced with the name of bungalow. A medical acquaintance has referred to these housing developments as *bungaloid growths*, and one wishes it were possible to take surgical action to excise them from the face of Scotland.

CARRICK

South of Ayr there is no industry to speak of, so there has been little despoliation of the villages. Indeed only Maybole and Girvan are big enough to be considered as towns, and as towns go, they are both small. Maybole is the traditional capital of Carrick, an old town where the town houses of the Kennedy kith and kin were located. It was once a place of many castles, but only the old castle at the foot of the High Street remains to remind us of the wild days of Kennedy rule. Maybole stands on a steep hillside

11

Kirkcudbright—solid walls and cobbled streets

looking out across Carrick countryside from which it derived its past prosperity. It once had agricultural machinery, tanning and shoemaking industries, but these have vanished and Maybole has known hard times of late. Now, much of the old decaying property has been swept away and replaced by council estates. And fortunately the town has been spared much of that bungalow development which has affected more prosperous places.

Girvan is basically a fishing port, although it has developed as a holiday resort and more recently as a small industrial centre. It is a quiet, unspoilt town, of a few wide streets lined with the sort of low cottages that one finds in the villages. Indeed, Girvan is merely a larger version of the other fishing villages—of Ballantrae, Turnberry, Maidens and Dunure.

All of the Carrick fishing villages are attractive, but Dunure is undisputedly the finest, because it stands at a point where the hills drop so steeply to the sea, that it resembles a Devon village with its picturesque harbour surrounded by houses and a ruined castle. And because the land rises sharply it is impossible to expand the village too much and spoil it.

The inland villages of Minishant, Kirkmichael, Crosshill and Straiton in the northern part of Carrick, and Barr and Colmonell in the south are little more than a single street of cottages, some with gardens but most opening straight on to the roadway. The cottages are rubble built or of rough stone, and once were thatched and whitewashed, but now are slated and tinted in pastel shades. Here and there a border of flowers has been planted between house and pavement to give some semblance of a garden, and in recent years business men from Ayr have begun to move to the villages and to commute to the town each day.

KYLE COAST TOWNS

When Burns went to Irvine to learn flax-dressing, he was not going to a minor burgh, but to one of Scotland's premier seaports and a place that claimed to be as old as Ayr. Yet in time, Irvine fell into eclipse as a port and declined despite the introduction of chemical manufacturers, engineering and shipbuilding. Now Irvine, together with Kilwinning and several villages, forms the basis of a new town which will be a great industrial centre with a population rising to over 100,000. As couthy little Irvine disappears, its Burns Club is strengthening its links with the past, and has established its own Burns Museum.

John Galt was born in Irvine, and although he left it as a small boy, the town made its mark on his character, for his novels give an impression of the place even as it is today—simple, solid, square, warm, and with a dry humour. Irvine is one of those places that retain their Scottishness despite all the Anglicizing influences around it. One hopes expansion will not spoil it.

The two towns between Irvine and Ayr are very different. Both Prestwick and Troon are grander places, with "grace-proud" faces turned towards the Firth of Clyde. The two are similar in many respects, but they differ in others. Both are domitory towns for Glasgow business men, yet they have a respectable amount of industry of their own. Both are holiday resorts with fine sandy beaches and championship golf courses. They are small towns, a mixture of grey and red stone houses which are well-maintained and attractive. Prestwick is the older of the two, with Bruce's Well at Kincase, where the Scottish king came to take the mineral waters, but of the two Troon is the more wealthy. Prestwick is a town of villas and cottages, but Troon is one of villas and great mansions, where some of the great industrial families of Glasgow have settled to be within easy reach of their factories, their sport and the countryside.

NEUKS O' KILLIE

Burns never actually lived in Kilmarnock, but he was a frequent visitor to the town and he had many friends there. Indeed, it was on the printing presses of John Wilson that the first edition of his poems—the Kilmarnock edition—was published. Even today, Kilmarnock takes more than a passing interest in Burns, for it is the headquarters of the Federation which links Burns Clubs throughout the world.

Kilmarnock is an old town, although it has little history of note. It was while fishing at Riccarton that Wallace had his encounter with English soldiers that forced him to find refuge in Leglen Woods. A thorn tree, known as the bickering bush, once marked the spot, but the only reminder of the incident which I could find on my last visit to Riccarton was a public house known as the Bickering Bush.

In Burns's day Kilmarnock was a town of handloom weavers who lived and worked in cottages as tightly packed in the many alleyways as peas in a pod. They were couthy people, and Burns had many friends among them—Robert Muir, whose early death grieved the poet greatly, John Goldie, and Thomas Samson the seed merchant, one of Burns's cronies at Sandy Patrick's public house. Tam was a keen sportsman, and this led Burns to write a mock elegy which delighted everyone except Samson himself. As it was recited, Samson cried, "Aye, but I'm no' deid yet." The protest prompted Burns to add the "Per Contra"

> Go, Fame, an' canter like a filly
> Thro' a' the streets an' neuks o' Killie,
> Tell ev'ry social, honest billie
>   To cease his grievin',
> For yet unskaith'd by Death's gleg gullie[1]
>   Tam Samson's leevin'.

Tam Samson was not the only butt of Burns's verse, for there were ministers quarrelling amongst themselves to be satirized and to inspire poetry. It was a quarrel between the dour minister of the High Kirk of Kilmarnock, John Russell, and Alexander Moodie of Riccarton that inspired "The Twa Herds":

[1] quick knife.

Sic two—O, do I live to see't?—
Sic famous two sud disagree't,
An' names like villain, hypocrite,
      Ilk ither gi'en[1]
While New Light herds wi' laughin' spite
      Say neither's liein'!

Then there was "The Ordination" based on the return of an
Auld Light minister to the Laigh Kirk in the town. After William
Lindsay, who is best remembered as the husband of Maggie
Lauder, and John Mutrie came James Mackinlay, an orthodox
minister of the old school who inspired Burns to comment:

Curst common-sense, that imp o' hell,
      Cam in wi' Maggie Lauder:
But Oliphant[2] aft made her yell,
An' Russell[2] sair misca'ed her;
This day Mackinlay taks the flail,
And he's the boy will blaud[3] her
He'll clap a shangan[4] on her tail
An' set the bairns to daud[5] her
      Wi' dirt this day.

Like the quarrelling ministers the alleys of Kilmarnock have
almost all vanished, and the few that remain are lined with shops
and smart cafes, for Ayrshire folk like their food. Industry is now
concentrated in great factories which do not enhance the town's
appearance, but Kilmarnock has attractive parts, especially where
the Dean water runs through a deep valley which is a public park.
However, Kilmarnock has its share of both bungalows and acres
of characterless council housing estates. But this is a fault which is
repeated in almost every town and village in the country.

[1] each other giving.
[2] ministers at the High Kirk.
[3] slap.
[4] cleft stick.
[5] hit.

INLAND KYLE

Tarbolton and Mauchline are the two places inland from Ayr which are most closely associated with Burns, and both have changed a lot in appearance since he knew them. Daddy Auld's kirk in Mauchline—"as ugly an old lump of consecrated stone as ever encumbered the earth"—has been replaced by a stately red church around which are buried many of Burns's family and acquaintances and, apart from the Bachelors' Club in Tarbolton, not a thatched cottage survives. Nevertheless much that was connected with the poet in both places remains—Gavin Hamilton's House, the Armours' house and Poosie Nancie's Inn. And at Mauchline there are cottages for elderly people, as a living memorial to the poet.

Burns overshadows everyone else in the Kyle, but Ochiltree is quietly proud of its own literary genius, George Douglas Brown, whose single work *The House With the Green Shutters* promised so much, had he not died at only thirty-four years of age. His birthplace is a cottage on the steep street of the village—literally the house with the green shutters. It is a typical Ayrshire village house, once a simple cottage with two small twelve paned windows flanking the door, and dormer windows added to turn the attic into bedrooms at a later date. The door and window lintels have been picked out in green paint, and because this is the birthplace of George Douglas Brown, green shutters have been added to the lower windows.

From the house with the green shutters, one looks across grey countryside to the upturned funnels of the Barony Pit at Auchinleck and on to Cumnock. This is the start of grey, upland Ayrshire, and the towns become grey upland towns, in which the bank is the most prosperous looking building. Both Cumnock and New Cumnock are unsmiling places, with little to attract the eye in either of them. The houses are solid enough, but here and there some have been demolished, leaving the town gap-toothed and uneven. One is not satisfied with the old, but neither is one happy

about the new fire station whose stark tower is out of harmony
with its surroundings.

NITHSDALE

Over the county boundary one is disappointed to find that
Kirkconnel has the same look of decay as the Cumnocks. Many
houses are ready to be demolished—as indeed is the township of
prefabricated houses that stands a little apart from the town. At
Sanquhar, things improve; here there is more prosperity, the
houses are better-kept, and the winding main street is crowned—
and crowded—by a charming old Council House. Burns often
passed through Sanquhar in the course of his revenue work and on
his way between Ellisland and Ayrshire, and there used to be a
medallion of the poet on the wall of a house opposite the Council
House. Charles Dougall, who wrote about the Burns Country
sixty years ago, met the man who lived in the house bearing the
medallion and this was the story of its origin.

"Weel, ye see," said the dweller in the house, "a man up at the
brickworks got an order for ane o' thae things, so he made twa;
an' says he tae me: 'Ye're a great Burns man, ye should stick this
up on the wa' o' yer hoose.' Weel, I kent it was an aul' hoose, and
some gret folk hea been conneckit wi't, an' he wisna' wantin'
mickle for't, sae I jist put it up, an' mony a ane has stoppit an'
glowr'd at it, I can tell ye."

As Dougall comments—It is thus that legends are made.

The next Nithsdale village is Thornhill, which had closer links
with Carlyle than with Burns, although exciseman Robert visited
the village often enough. Thornhill is one of those villages which
one encounters unexpectedly and remembers long afterwards. It
comprises two wide streets which form a cross, and each of which
is lined with lime trees planted over a hundred years ago by the
Duke of Buccleuch of the day.

QUEEN OF THE SOUTH

Dumfries calls itself the Queen of the South and few would

dispute that cognomen. Although the town has far more reminders of Burns than Ayr has, it tries to retain its identity as a place of some importance—county town and market town—for a wide region. The early settlement was a defensive one, on a great loop of the River Nith, around which grew a town which received its charter as a royal burgh in 1186. Devorgilla built a bridge and religious houses there, and it was there that Bruce stabbed the Red Comyn and set himself on the way to kingship. As in Ayr most of the ancient town of Dumfries has vanished. Indeed, the town's strongest links are literary rather than historical. Burns lived and died in it, Allan Cunningham, author of "A Wet Sheet and a Flowing Sea" is commemorated in St. Michael's Church, and James Barrie, the author of *Peter Pan*, went to school at Dumfries Academy.

The Burns links are strongest, though. His house is a solid two-storeyed red building that gives the lie to any tale of poverty. It was the home of a man accustomed to living comfortably, and visitors may catch a glimpse of the background against which he lived and died, for the room in which he wrote so many of his songs and the bedroom where he died are preserved as they were in his time.

No distance away is the kirkyard where the bard lies in a splendid tomb containing a marble sculpture depicting him standing at the plough while the muse of Coila throws her mantle over him. It perpetuates the impression of a humble ploughman that Burns allowed to be put about during his lifetime. Although Dumfries gave the poet a hero's funeral he was buried in a simple grave in the north-west corner of St. Michael's Churchyard, and it was only twenty years later that his remains were moved to the splendid tomb in the middle of the churchyard.

Much that Burns knew can still be seen in Dumfries—St. Michael's Church itself, the eighteenth-century Midsteeple in the middle of the High Street as a challenge to twentieth-century traffic, the Globe Inn and the Hole I' The Wa' where he drank and did a lot more besides, and the beautiful eighteenth-century Theatre Royal where he was often among the audience.

Like most other towns in the South-west, Dumfries has been tidied up in recent years and its shopping centre is prosperous and well-kept. Except for the narrow crowded Friars Vennel the streets are mostly spacious with a fountain playing at one end of the High Street and Burns sitting thoughtfully on his plinth at the other. Ayr turns its back on its river, but Dumfries faces down to the Nith where wide esplanades with the evocative names Whitesands and Dockhead run along the river bank. Here the Nith runs beneath Devorgilla's old bridge and newer bridges, and rumbles over a weir. On the other bank stands Maxwelltown, once a burgh in its own right, but now part of the county town. Dumfries is a compact town, but Maxwelltown spreads itself out into great wandering housing developments of Lochside and Lincluden which run almost to the walls of Lincluden Abbey.

THE STEWARTRY

If Dumfries is Queen of the South, then Kirkcudbright is Queen of the Solway coast. It is typical of every other town and village in the Stewartry—picturesque, colourful and exuding charm from every cottage.

Kirkcudbright was once a great seaport, situated on the broad estuary of the River Dee, and well placed to trade with the transatlantic colonies, but its old harbour has been filled in many years ago. Before it became a seaport, it was a fortress, but the original castle has long vanished also. The tall ruin of Maclellan's Castle which dominates the town is a comparative newcomer, less than four hundred years old. Much of Kirkcudbright dates from the end of the seventeenth century and the early years of the eighteenth —which makes it older than the majority of houses in other parts of South-west Scotland.

Among those which have survived for two-and-a-half centuries is Broughton House, where artist E. A. Hornel made his home, and which he bequeathed to the town together with his paintings and books. Another survivor is the building which housed Paul

Jones's employers before he had to flee to join the rebels on the other side of the Atlantic and involve himself in exploits which made him one of the first heroes of the U.S.A.

The seventeenth-century Tolbooth at the end of the High Street also remains, as forbidding today as it ever was in its three hundred years of existence. The little spire which surmounts the eastern end of the building is made of stones from Dundrennan Abbey.

Kirkcudbright was made popular during this century by Hornel and a succession of artists who restored the old houses, and lived in them and painted them. Kirkcudbright exploits its reputation as an artist's paradise, but it is by no means an artificial centre of the arts—Kirkcudbright is the home of working artists, and the holidaymakers who visit it feel that they are sharing in this work.

Inland there are only two towns—the quarrying town of Dalbeattie, which is the best advertisement for its own magnificent Criffel granite, and Castle Douglas, a little town picturesquely placed on the edge of Carlingwark Loch. The other villages are no more than a few houses gathered in the folds of the hills—a few settlements running from Gatehouse of Fleet on the Solway through charmingly named villages of Twynholm, Lauriston, Crossmichael, Crocketford, Balmaclellan New Galloway, and Dalry to Carsphairn on the Ayrshire border. Most of the villages comprise a single street of neat cottages fronted with neatly kept flower beds. Galloway folk have complemented the work of nature in their villages; here the mark of man is least offensive.

Each place commemorates its famous sons—Old Mortality at Balmaclellan, S. R. Crockett at Laurieston where he was born and where he died, and Alexander Murray on the road from Clatteringshaws Loch to Newton Stewart. You may miss the ruined shepherd's cottage called Dunkitterick where Murray was born, but you will certainly see the monument to him high on the hill not far away. Alexander Murray was a shepherd's son, born in 1775, who taught himself eastern and African languages, and, a

typical Scottish lad o' pairts, won a place at Edinburgh University.
When a letter arrived from an Abyssinian potentate in 1811 it had
to be sent to Murray, who was by then a minister in Galloway, to
be translated. The following year he became Professor of Oriental
Languages at Edinburgh University, but he died in 1813.

WIGTOWNSHIRE

At Newton Stewart one crosses from a peaceful Kirkcudbright
village into a busy little Wigtownshire town, whose appearance
suggests few frills and fancy architectural devices. Its long neat
streets are flanked with two storey buildings which are simple and
functional; warm rather than aesthetically noteworthy. But, of
course, the same could be said of almost every other place in the
South-west.

Newton Stewart is an old town; Stranraer, at the other end of
the county is a new one. It has grown up over the last century
since the terminal port for the Northern Ireland ferry was moved
from Portpatrick to a more sheltered harbour at the head of
Loch Ryan. As a new town it has plenty of pleasant enough buildings but few that are outstanding, and like Newton Stewart it is a
functional place rather than a beautiful one.

The smaller towns and hamlets are more charming—Wigtown,
Whithorn, the Isle of Whithorn and Portpatrick are exciting little
places, whose bright houses perfectly express the character of the
people who inhabit them. The leavening of the Wigtownshire
character is much in evidence, and one could hardly imagine these
gaily coloured cottages in stolid Kyle or even Dumfries. As elsewhere, much has been done to stop the decay of the immediate
pre-war and wartime years, and the process of improvement has
gained momentum in the past decade. Nowhere in the South-west
is the work of man more in harmony with the work of nature.
Nowhere is the mark of man more pleasing.

XII

IMMORTAL MEMORY

Was it the rhythmic moving of the handloom? Or merely an outlet for active minds as hands busied themselves weaving cloth? Whatever the reason, the traditional weaving districts of Ayrshire and Renfrewshire have produced more than their share of poets. Few of these village bards had great merit; some had none at all, but none surely were ever as bad as this often-quoted sample would suggest:

> Ae nicht three men tae oor door cam'
> They asked for tea; I gied them ham.
> Says I, "Are ye frae Mauchline cam?"
> Said they, "We am".

Although this verse has been attributed to one of the many Mauchline poets, it has also been quoted with Paisley substituted for Mauchline. The truth is that it was used by one town against another, and any name could be made to fit.

Every town and village had its poets—they still have, as the columns of the local weekly newspapers testify. The vast majority of these versifiers live and die in obscurity—a fate which does not distress them unduly for they do not write for fame or money, but to satisfy themselves and to give their neighbours pleasure. And by these standards they are immensely successful.

Burns has spurred scores of his countrymen to verse over the

last century and a half, but even in his own time there were other
verse-makers in Ayrshire. The best-known of his contemporary
poetasters is David Sillar, one of his Tarbolton companions, to
whom Burns addressed two epistles. One of these "Epistles to
Davie" gives a clue to the reason why the people of the South-west
make rhymes. Burns wrote:

> Leeze me on rhyme![1] It's aye a treasure
> My chief, amaist[2] my only pleasure;
>
> At hame, a-fiel', at work or leisure
>   The Muse, poor hizzie!
> Tho' rough·an' raploch[3] be her measure,
>   She's seldom lazy.

In a phrase, they rhyme because they enjoy it.

Their verse serves many purposes—to compliment or comfort a
friend, to comment on some important event in history, or just to
record a trivial local incident. They are minstrels of the common
folk, and as their verse loses its topicality, it vanishes into obscurity.
And yet one finds among all the day-to-day verse, some pieces of
merit. When David Ramsay turned that favourite Scottish Psalm,
the Twenty-Third, into Lowland dialect, he produced something
which will reach to the heart of every Scot. In his hands "The
Lord is my Shepherd" becomes . . .

> The Lord tae me has aye been kin'.
>   A richt guid Herd, I trow;
> My wan'erin' feet has guided aft
>   By mony a heigh and howe.
>
> Doon by some bonnie burnie side
>   A bield for me He'd mak'.
> If wav'rin' whiles, gied me His han'
>   Lest I gaed aff the track.

[1] rhyme is dear to me.
[2] almost.
[3] coarse cloth.

> When I gang roun the hin'most bend
> Trauchled and unco lame,
> His crook I'll see held oot tae me
> Wi' it He'll lead me hame.
>
> On guid plain fare He fed me weel,
> My coggie ne'er was toom;
> The wolf aye keepit frae my door,
> Watched owre me late and sune.
>
> Wi' a' things guid He wasna' scrimp
> If keepin' by His side;
> And in that bucht ayont the clouds
> Wi' Him I fain wad bide.

Burns provided the impetus for many poets, and since his day places like Kilmarnock and Irvine have produced scores of poets. In Irvine the poets had a distinctly religious bent, and the results of their labours are to be found in the Church of Scotland Hymn Book. Anne Ross Cousin, was a wife of the Irvine manse when she wrote "The Sands of Time are Sinking", and James Montgomery has more than a dozen hymns in the Scottish hymnal.

In the make-up of the South-western Scot there is much sentiment and sentimentality, which is strongly evident in his poetry. Indeed, that is often the part of a poet's work that endures in these parts. For example, although the sonnets of Kirkconnel poet Alexander Anderson are already forgotten, many people can quote from his *Cuddle Doon* poems.

> The bairnies cuddle doon at nicht
> Wi' muckle faucht an' din,
> O, try and sleep, ye waukrife rogues,
> Your faither's comin' in.

And, of course, 'hame' figures prominently in the poems, with Allan Cunningham's exile's song as the epitomy of all the others:

> Hame, hame, hame, O hame, fain wad I be—
> O hame, hame, hame, to my ain countree!

Over a century and a half a long procession of poets from Keats to Samual Marshak, the Russian translator of Burns, have made the tour from Alloway to St. Michael's Churchyard to pay homage to his genius, and to find inspiration. Some were less successful than others. In 1818, Keats visited Burns's Cottage, which was then an inn, but the landlord's ignorance of the Bard so appalled him that he could only write a poor sonnet. "The flat dog, made me write a flat sonnet," Keats complained.

At Mossgiel, Wordsworth fared better:

> "There!" said a stripling, pointing with meet pride
> Towards a low roof with green trees half concealed,
> "Is Mossgiel farm; and that's the very field
> Where Burns ploughed up the Daisy." Far and wide
> A plain below stretched seaward, while, descried
> Above sea-clouds, the Peaks of Arran rose;
> And by that simple notice, the repose
> Of earth, sky, sea, and air was vivified.
> Beneath 'the random bield of clod or stone'
> Myriads of Daisies have shone forth in flower
> Near the lark's nest, and in their natural hour
> Have passed away less happy than the One
> That by the unwilling ploughshare did to prove
> The tender charm of Poetry and of Love.

A more recent visitor to Mossgiel had an encounter which came closer to that of Keats at Alloway than to Wordsworth's. Instead of a proud stripling, he found an old man standing beside a gate— probably of that same field where the daisy was ploughed up— and as there are two farms named Mossgiel, he asked: "Which is Burns's Mossgiel?"

The old man thought carefully, shook his head, and replied, "I dinna ken, but it isna' this ane, for it's Wyllie bides here."

For the old man, Mossgiel is a twentieth-century Ayrshire farm where men follow the plough, and not a mausoleum to an eighteenth-century poet who paused to commiserate with the daisy and the mouse when he disturbed them. And yet, surely no

Scot can isolate himself from Burns as easily or as completely as that. The whole country is a memorial to the Bard, for it was through Burns that its nationhood was reborn.

During the second half of the eighteenth century, Scotland was filled with great writers, philosophers, engineers and architects, for this was the Golden Age that saw the creation of the classical New Town of Edinburgh. At the same time, it was an age when the old Scotland was rapidly vanishing into the maw of England, and the Scottish nation was in danger of being wiped out. This was no new process; it had been going on for two centuries, begun by the Reformation which allied Scotland to England instead of France, continued by James VI and his followers when the Scottish king fell heir to the English crown in 1603, and completed when the Parliaments of the two countries were united in 1707. Fortunately, a handful of men emerged to save Scotland's lore and language, and even more fortunately, among those men was one genius—Robert Burns.

Burns was so much a man of the people—the rich and poor, the unpolished and the sophisticated alike—that he was able to express accurately the feelings of every class of society in the country. He was able to write poetry which is timeless; as relevant to our age as to his own. Every tenet which he held and every concept which he expressed belongs as much to our period in time as to the eighteenth century, which is why so many of the thoughts which he expressed have become platitudes—In 1780 a man was a man for a' that; he still is. Two hundred years ago, the Burns family knew well enough that the best laid schemes "gang aft agley"; many Ayrshire farming folk who live by the whim of the weather or the welfare state know that schemes still go "agley". And if only some power would enable us to see ourselves as others see us, it would save us from many a blunder and foolish notion. In the changing Scotland of Burns's time, that was equally true.

These great truths are expressed by Burns with unmatched skill. Think of the picture of the Kirk at Lamington that he conjured up in four simple lines:

Dumfries—life revolves round the Midsteeple

> As cauld a wind as ever blew,
> A caulder kirk, and in't but few;
> A caulder preacher never spak;—
> Ye'se a' be het ere I come back.

Four lines to describe kirk, congregation and minister! Surely that is craftsmanship of the highest order, and it is this combination of basic commonsense and skill of expression that has made him the most vital poet of any age or any nation. It is this rare fusion that has made him as popular in Moscow, Russia, as in Moscow, Ayrshire.

Nor should one forget the glorious songs which he gave to the world. I have already referred to these, so now I will single out one which probably means more to a greater number of people than any other song in the world. "Auld Lang Syne" has become a universal song of parting . . .

> Should auld acquaintance be forgot,
> And never brought to mind?
> Should auld acquaintance be forgot,
> For auld lang syne.

Perhaps the most beautiful verses of the song are those which are least often sung, when Burns recalls the happy summer days that are gone:

> We twa hae run about the braes,
> And pu'd the gowans fine;
> But we've wander'd mony a weary foot
> Sin' auld lang syne.

> We twa hae paidled i' the burn,
> From morning sun till dine;
> But seas between us braid hae roar'd
> Sin' auld lang syne.

Every man has his own vision of the scene which these two verses conjure up, but for me, the burn is the one which flows

12

"Here pause—and thro' the starting tear survey this grave . . ."—
Burns's Mausoleum, Dumfries

gently into the river Doon just below Minishant, and the braes
are the Whinnie Knowe above the village. And I never read or
sing these verses without feeling the warmth of childhood
summers there more than a generation ago.

That is why I, like the whole world, am glad to sing:

> For auld lang syne, my dear,
>   For auld lang syne,
> We'll tak a cup o' kindness yet,
>   For auld lang syne.

Scotland still reaps the harvest of that genius who spent a mere
thirty-seven summers on her soil, and her people never tire of
expressing their gratitude to him. To southerners, the annual
gatherings of the 25th of January have a touch of the comic about
them. The Burns Supper seems little more than an opportunity to
drink whisky, and tell the world how Scottish we all are. To the
Scot, however, it is a time to take stock of himself, and a chance
to honour the man who helped his homeland rediscover its nationhood. That is why Burns Night is an even more important date
than St. Andrew's Night or any other night of the Scottish
year. On that night Scotsmen throughout the world turn their
thoughts to home, and are united by the overwhelmingly powerful bond of patriotism. Today, when the spirit of nationalism is
stronger than it has been for many years Burns is again the prince
who rallies even the faint-hearted to the cause. Together they sing

> Wha for Scotland's King and law,
> Freedom's sword will strongly draw,
> Free man stand, or free man fa'!
>   Let him follow me!

Who cares whether that was the rallying call for Bannockburn
in 1314, or an exhortation to preserve freedom in the eighteenth
century. To today's Scot it belongs to his own age. And to to-
morrow's Scot it will be equally relevant.

No Scot can resist such a battle cry.

Lay the proud usurper low!
Tyrants fall in every foe!
Liberty's in every blow!
Let us do, or die!

Burns belongs to the whole Scottish nation—indeed, he belongs
to the world—but no other people can feel the same kinship
towards him as do those of us who were born and bred in the same
countryside. On January 25th we do not honour a great man set
apart, although we do revere him greatly, but we pay homage
to one of our own relations—to someone who walked the same
roads, ploughed the same fields, and spoke the same language as
we do. And because Burns was made by same accidents of
geography and incidents of history as have made us, we feel that
at least in part we are the same as he was. In all of us is something
of the trauchled worker, the carefree roisterer, the earnest father,
and the cheery companion. Alas we lack the genius to express our
personality and feelings in the timeless language of Robert Burns.
Even today the South Western Scot remains close to the hard
and simple life of the country, and in himself he sees much of the
cotter of "The Cotter's Saturday Night". On a winter's afternoon
one still sees the opening of the poem:

November chill blaws loud wi' angry sough;
    The short'ning winter-day is near a close;
The miry beasts retreating frae the pleugh;
    The black'ning trains o' craws to their repose;
The toil-worn Cotter frae his labour goes,
    This night his weekly moil is at an end,
Collects his spades, his mattocks, and his hoes,
    Hoping the morn in ease and rest to spend,
And weary, o'er the moor, his course does hameward bend.

This is the way of life our fathers knew, and even if we are
town-dwellers now, we live in towns small enough to remind
us of the country way of life close by. The scene is altered only
in detail—the 'miry beasts' have been replaced by a muddy tractor,

but the cotter is weary at the week's end, and he looks forward to a few hours of relaxation with his family.

Small wonder then that Burns's poems bridge two centuries so easily.

Small wonder, too, that the Burns Country is a lovingly tended memorial to the Bard. The traveller comes here to visit the stone and lime relics of Burns's time—the cottage at Alloway, the neat farms of Kyle, the kirkyard of Mauchline, the lovely old farmstead of Ellisland, the tall red house at Dumfries, and the sparkling white Mausoleum—but he finds that the Burns Country does not live solely in the past. The Burnsiana may be part of the scene but so too are the great runways of Scotland's only international Airport at Prestwick, the Imperial Chemical Industries complex at Irvine and Dumfries, the bakery that sells Land O' Burns bread, and the factory that manufactures Tam O' Shanter hones to sharpen knives in every part of the world.

And as in Burns's time the South-west of Scotland is passing through a disturbing phase of transition. Mining is shrinking, and threatens to shrink even further, and farming is changing, too, as the tenant farmer is forced to yield his land so that it can be formed into more economically viable units. All this forces countrymen into the town—for one must remember that even the miners in these parts are countrymen—and it makes for a feeling of insecurity. The pity is that there is no Robert Burns to plead their cause.

Greater changes are yet to come, and no one can predict what these will be. We know of the great new town that is to be built at Irvine within a few years, but we cannot tell whether the Solway Firth will ever be dammed and a large port built there. Nor can we know whether Edinburgh and Glasgow businessmen will one day live in the Stewartry and commute to their offices each day by helicopters or hovercraft.

Robert Burns would feel at home and among friends in the intense green country if he were to return to Ayrshire today. He would stravaige the countryside, penning poems of praise to his friends, wicked epigrams on his enemies. He would fight for the rights of man without malice, and he would love his friends and respect his enemies.

And on parting he would say again:

> Farewell, old Coila's hills and dales,
> Her heathy moors and winding vales;
> The scenes where wretched fancy roves,
> Pursuing past unhappy loves!
> Farewell, my friends! Farewell, my foes!
> My peace with these, my love with those;
> The bursting tears my heart declare,
> Farewell, the bonnie banks of Ayr!

INDEX

A

Abbeys, 84–86
Adam, Robert, 154
Afton Water, 51
Agriculture, 118–23, 156, 157
Ailsa Craig, 15, 40, 49–51
Ailsa, Marquis of, 76, 154
Aird's Moss, 89
Alexander, Sir William, of Menstrie, 123
Alloway, 16, 17, 18, 37, 46, 47, 148, 156, 157, 158, 160, 176, 180
— Auld Kirk, 47, 139, 155, 158
— Mill, 18
Anderson, Alexander, 174
Annals of the Parish, 93
Annbank, 45
Annick Water, 44
App, Water of, 49
Arbigland, 62
Ardrossan, 45, 123
Armour, Jean, 29, 30, 31, 32, 34, 35, 51, 53, 160
Arran, 15, 101
Auchendrane, 47, 75, 76
Auchincruive, 45, 77, 122
Auchinleck, 42, 77, 166
Auld, Dr. William ('Daddy'), 25, 29, 37, 95, 166
"Auld Lang Syne", 32, 105, 177

Auld Lichts, 25, 94, 95
Auldgirth Bridge, 52
Ayr, 18, 19, 37, 42, 43, 44, 45, 47, 48, 72, 75, 86, 87, 99, 100, 102, 109, 110, 111, 116, 121, 123, 128, 133, 145, 147, 150, 152, 154, 155, 157
— Auld Brig of, 45, 160
— New Bridge, 45, 160
— Heads of, 48
— River, 30, 44, 45, 46, 47, 104, 105, 133, 160, 181
Ayrshire, 15, 30, 37, 39, 41, 42–51, 59, 65, 66, 71, 72, 74, 79, 85, 86, 89, 95, 96, 99, 101, 109, 113, 114, 119, 122, 123, 126, 128, 129, 133, 134, 136, 146, 147, 150, 151, 167, 174, 175, 176
— Cattle, 120

B

Bachelors' Club, 22, 166
Bailie, family of, 77
Ballantrae, 49, 65, 124, 162
Balliol, John, 62, 100
Balmaclellan, 61, 88, 89, 170
Bannockburn, 56, 101, 102
Baron of Buchlyvie, 121
Bargany, 74, 79
Barr, 126
Barrie, James, 168

Barskimming, 45
Benane Head, 49
Benyellary, 59
Bladnoch, River, 57, 84
Blair, family of, 77
Boswell, family of, 73, 110
Boswell, Alexander, 159
Boyd, family of, 77
Broughton House, 63, 169
Broun, Agnes, 16
Brow, 35
Brown Carrick Hill, 48
Brown, Richard, 24, 37
Bruce, Edward, 102
— Marjorie, 57, 103, 160
— Robert the, 16, 56, 57, 62, 83, Ch. VI
Bruce, The, 102
"Bruce Before Bannockburn", 105
Bruce Stone, 56, 60, 102
Buccleuch, Dukes of, 52, 77, 154, 167
Buchan, Mrs. 'Luckie', 91-2
Buchanites, 91-2
Burnes, William, 16, 17, 18, 22, 157, 158
Burns, Gilbert, 18, 19, 20, 21
— Robert, Ch. I, 45, 46, 47, 52, 53, 55, 92, 94, 95, 103, 108, 117, 123, 132, 151, 153, 160, 163, Ch.XII
— Rev. Thomas, 95
Burns Cottage, 39, 176
Burns's Monument, 139, 157-8, 159
Burrow Head, 67
Bute, Marquis of, 77

C
Caerlaverock, 77, 88, 153
Cairn Edward Forest, 102
Cairnryan, 65, 68, 140, 141
Cairnsmore of Carsphairn, 59
Cairnsmore of Fleet, 59

Cameron, Meg, 31
Campbell, family of, 74, 76, 79, 153
Campbell, Mary (Highland Mary), 30, 45, 160
Candida Casa, 67
Cardoness Castle, 64, 153
Carlyle, family of, 77
Carlyle, Thomas, 63, 64, 167
Carpet manufacture, 138
Carrick, 16, 47, 71, 78, 101, 104, 111, 116, 125, 137, 158, 161-2
Carrick, Earl of, 100, 101
Carrick Forest, 59
Carsfad Power Station, 61
Carsluith Castle, 64, 153
Carsphairn, 59, 170
Carsphairn Lane, 61
Cassillis, 47, 153, 155
Cassillis, Earl of, 74, 154
Castle Douglas, 61, 120, 170
Castle Kennedy, 79, 84
Cathcart, family of, 76, 79
Catrine, 45, 136
Cessnock Water, 44
Changue Forest, 59
Clatteringshaws Dam, 60, 61
Closeburn, 92
Clow, Jenny, 31
Clyde, Firth of, 15, 18, 48, 70, 147, 163
Coal-mining, 51, 128-33
Cockburn, Lord, 110
Cole, King, 73
Comyn John (Red Comyn), 100, 101, 168
Corrie, John, 89
"Cotter's Saturday Night, The", 36, 179
Cousin, Anne Ross, 174
Covenanters, 87-91, 108
Coyle, Water of, 45

Crammag Head, 59
Crawford, family of, 47, 76, 110, 153
Cree, River, 56, 57, 64, 65, 66, 67, 76
Creetown, 59, 62, 63, 140
Crichton, family of, 77
Criffel, 58, 62
Crocketford, 61, 170
Crockett, S. R., 47, 54, 56, 75
Crosshill, 48, 162
Crossmichael, 170
Crossraguel Abbey, 50, 85, 128, 155
Croy Brae, 48
Culroy, 48
Culzean Castle, 40, 48, 49, 75, 154, 155
Cumnock, New, 42, 43, 51, 52, 166
— Old, 42, 43, 52, 134, 166
Cunningham, 16, 77, 102, 104, 119, 137
Cunningham, Allan, 168, 174
Curleywee Hill, 60
Curling Stones, 50

D

Dailly, 48, 101, 128
Dalbeattie, 58, 63, 140, 170
Dalmellington, 43, 46, 51, 129, 152
Dalry, 61, 170
Dalrymple, family of, 78, 110
— William, 95
Dalrymple, 47, 79, 115, 156
Dalswinton, 53
Darvel, 44, 136
David I, King, 63
David II, King, 83, 103
Davidson, Betty, 19, 106
"Death and Dr. Hornbrook", 22
Dee, Loch, 60
— Water of, 57, 60, 61, 63, 160
Devorgilla, 56, 62, 86, 168
Dick Hattrick's Cave, 64

Distinthill, 64
Doon, Brig' O', 158, 159
— Loch, 46, 59, 60, 61, 102, 153
— River, 42, 43, 45, 46, 47, 48, 60, 96, 104, 105, 111, 157, 160, 178
Doonholm, 16, 47
Dornal, Loch, 65
Douglas, family of, 77
Douglas, George, 109, 166
Douglas, William of Drumlanrig, 79
Douglas, William of Fingland, 78
Drumclog, 44, 89
Drumlanrig Castle, 52, 77, 154
Drummore, 69
Drummurchie, 75
Dumfries, 31, 34, 35, 37, 39, 51, 53-4, 56, 58, 61, 62, 77, 85, 86, 88, 109, 112, 113, 123, 139, 149, 152, 153, 167-9, 171
Dumfriesshire, 39, 42, 51-4, 71, 72, 113, 119, 126, 128, 135, 144, 153
Dundeuch, 59
Dundonald, 137, 153
Dundrennan Abbey, 63, 84, 155, 170
Dungeon, Long Loch of, 60
— Round Loch of, 60
Dunlop, Mrs., 30, 35, 37
Dunlop, William, 121
Dunscore, 87
Dunure, 74, 124, 162

E

Earlston Power Station, 61
Edinburgh, 19, 24, 30, 176
Eisenhower, Dwight D., 155
Electric Brae (Croy Brae), 48
Ellisland, 31, 32, 34, 51, 52, 149, 167
Enoch Hill, 51
Enoch, Loch, 60
"Epistle to William Simson", 105

F

Falkirk, Battle of, 56, 100
Fenwick Water, 44
Fergus, Lord of Galloway, 63, 78, 83, 84, 85
Fisher, William ('Holy Willie'), 25, 29, 37
Fishing Industry, 124-5
Fleet, Water of, 57
Forestry, 125-7
Fullarton family, 11

G

Galloway, Earls of, 79
Galloway, 16, 30, 39, 40, 42, 48, 54, Ch. III, 70, 71, 72, 78, 83, 89, 90, 102, 109, 116, 126, 137, 140, 149, 151
— Burn, 49
— Cattle, 120
Galston, 44
Galt, John, 92, 93, 163
Garnock, River, 43, 44, 128
Garpel Water, 45
Gatehouse-of-Fleet, 55, 62, 63
Girvan, 41, 49, 50, 125, 133, 139, 154, 162
Girvan, Water of, 43, 48, 128
Glasgow, 39, 45, 110, 123, 140, 148, 152, 163
Glasgow and West of Scotland Agricultural College, 122
Glen Water, 44
Glenapp, 49, 56
Glenbuck, 45
Glengarnock, 43, 133
Glenhead, Long Loch of, 60
— Round Loch of, 60
Glenlee Power Station, 60, 61
Glenlochan Barrage, 61
Glenluce, 66, 67, 153

Glenluce Abbey, 85
Glen Trool Martyrs, 90
Glen Trool Village, 57, 126
Gordon family, 74, 79, 80
Gordon, James, of Lochinvar, 79
"Green Grow the Rashes O", 24
Greenock Water, 45
Grey Man, The, 75

H

Hadyard Hill, 101
Hamilton, Gavin, 24, 25, 26, 30, 95
"Holy Fair, The", 25, 27-9
"Holy Willie's Prayer", 25-7, 36
Hornel, E. A., 63, 169, 170
House With The Green Shutters, The, 109, 166
Hunter-Blair family, 76
Hurlford, 44
Hydro-electric Power Scheme, 60-1

I

Irongray, 90
Irvine, 23, 24, 37, 40, 43, 99, 104, 105, 123
Irvine, River, 42, 43, 44, 45, 99, 104, 105, 123

J

James I, King, 83
James II, King, 83
James VI, King, 87, 176
Johnstone family, 77
Jones, John Paul, 54, 56, 62, 169

K

Kells, Rhinns of, 58, 60, 61
Ken, Loch, 60, 61, 126
— River, 60
Kendoon Reservoir, 61
Kennedy family, 47, 73-6, 78, 79, 84, 85, 87, 110, 153, 161

Kennedy, Sir Gilbert, 74
— Gilbert of Bargany, 75
— Abbot Quintin, 86
— Sir Thomas, 75
Kennedy's Pass, 49
Kilmarnock, 30, 37, 44, 71, 92, 95, 99,
    109, 133, 134, 135, 136, 138, 145,
    150, 151, 163-5
Kilpatrick, Nelly, 20
Kilwinning, 133, 163
Kippford, 62, 149
Kirkbean, 62
Kirkcolm, 68
Kirkconnel, 52, 167
Kirkcudbright, 55, 61, 62, 63, 123,
    152, 169, 170
— Stewartry of, 39, 42, 49, 56, 58,
    59-64, 66, 111, 112, 113, 119
Kirkmadrine, 82
Kirkmaiden, 69, 82
Kirkmichael (Ayrshire), 48, 162
Kirkmichael (Dumfriesshire), 113
Kirkoswald, 21, 37, 111, 124, 155
"Kirk's Alarm, The," 95
Kirriereoch, 45, 59
Kirroughtree Forest, 59
Knox, John, 86, 89
Kyle, 16, 18, 40, 42, 44, 47, 48, 74, 76,
    99, 102, 104, 107, 109, 117, 119,
    137, 153, 160, 162-7, 171, 180

L

Lace-making, 44
Lady Isle, 15
Lamachan Hill, 60
Larg Hill, 60
Latinus Stone, 82
Laurie, Annie, 78
Lauriston, 170
Lawson, Rev. Roderick, 50
Leglen Woods, 99

Lincluden Abbey, 54, 85, 169
Lochfoot, 89
Lochlie, 22, 24
Lochmaben, 153
Logan House, 69
Logan Water, 44
Loudon, Sir Hew, 74
Loudon Hall, 160
Loudon Hill, 102
Luce, Water of, 57, 65, 66, 67; Cross
    Water, 66; Main Water, 66
Luce Bay, 42, 64, 67, 68, 82
Lugar Water, 45

M

Mabery, Loch, 65
Macadam, John Loudon, 150, 151
Macaterick, Loch, 60
McCulloch family, 79, 153
MacDowalls of Garthland, 74, 79, 101
Machars, 67-8, 79, 119
Macintyre, Group Captain D., 134,
    152
Mackinlay, James, 165
McLauchlan, Margaret, 90
Maclehose, Mrs. Agnes, 31, 160
Maclellan family, 79, 80
Maclellan, Sir Thomas of Bombie, 63,
    79
Maclellan's Castle, 63, 153
Maidenkirk, 56
Maidens, 124, 125
Mary Queen of Scots, 63, 83, 84, 153
Mauchline, 24, 25, 29, 44, 152, 166,
    172, 180
Maxwell family, 77, 85
Maxwelltown, 54, 78, 85, 169
Maybole, 42, 48, 50, 59, 75, 86, 89,
    111
Merrick, 49, 58, 59, 60, 61
Minishant, 48, 115, 137, 156, 162, 178

Minnigaff, 66, 126
Minnoch, Water of, 66
Moan, Loch, 66
Moniaive, 52, 78, 152
Monkton, 77, 95
Monreith Bay, 67
Montgomerie family, 77
Moors, 64, 65
Mossgiel, 24, 29, 44, 51, 175
Mount Oliphant, 17, 18, 20, 22
Muirkirk, 89
Mull of Galloway, 57, 58, 69, 123
Mulldonach, 60, 102
Murdoch, John, 18
Mure family, 47
Mure, John, of Auchendrane, 75
Mure, Walter, of Cloncarid, 75
Murray, Alexander, 54
Murray family, 77
Mutrie, John, 165
"My Nanie O", 24, 55

N
National Trust for Scotland, 154,
    155
Neldricken, Loch, 60
Ness Glen, 46
New Abbey, 62, 86
New Galloway, 61, 102, 126, 170
New Lichts, 25, 94
New Luce, 66
Newmilns, 44, 136
Newton-on-Ayr, 94, 160
Newton Stewart, 40, 58, 59, 66, 67,
    137, 170
Nick of the Balloch, 59
Ninian, St., 54, 56, 64, 67, 81–3
Nith, River, 51, 54, 57, 84, 86, 168,
    169
Nithsdale, 51, 52, 77, 154, 167

O
Ochiltree, 43, 105, 109, 114, 166
Ochiltree, Loch, 65, 66
"Of A' The Airts", 32
Old Mortality, 88, 89
Orchardton Tower, 153

P
Paisley, 29, 85
Palnure Burn, 67
Park, Castle of, 153
Patna, 46, 47
Paton, Elizabeth, 29, 35, 36
Penkhill, 66
Penwhirn Reservoir, 65
Peter Pan, 168
Physgill Glen, 82
Poems Chiefly in the Scottish Dialect, 30
Poosie Nancy, 37
Portpatrick, 58, 69, 72, 74, 152, 171
Port William, 57, 67
Prestwick, 42, 43, 74, 95, 147, 148,
    155, 160, 163
Prestwick International Airport, 15,
    134, 152

R
Railways, 151–2
Ramsay, David, 123, 175
Recawr, Loch, 60
"Red, Red Rose, A", 33
Reformation, 67, 77, 78, 83, 84, 85,
    86, 96
Reid family, 77
Religion, Ch. V
Rhinns of Galloway, 40, 64, 68, 69,
    82
Riccarton, 95, 99, 164
Robert II, King, 153
Rockcliffe, 62, 149
Roland, Lord of Galloway, 78, 84, 85

Ross, Sir John, 65
Ryan, Loch, 64, 65, 68, 140, 171

S
St. Mary's Isle, 62
St. Ninian's Chapel, 155
Saltcoats, 128, 131
Samson, Thomas, 164
Sandhead, 69
Saulseat, 84
Sanquhar, 52, 77, 128, 135, 167
"Scots Wha Hae", 55, 106
Scots Musical Museum, 32
Scott, Lady John, 78
— Sir Walter, 47, 55, 79, 88
Scottish Women's Rural Institute, 143-4
Select Scottish Airs, 32
Selkirk, Earl of, 55, 62
Shalloch-on-Minnoch, 49, 59
Sillar, David, 22, 23, 137, 175
Solway Firth, 16, 35, 40, 42, 47, 57, 58, 62, 63, 67, 123
Sorbie, 67
Sorn, 45, 150
South of Scotland Electricity Board, 60
Stair, 45, 133
Stair, Earls of, 78
Statistical Account, First, 113, 135, 150
— New, 135, 156
— Third, 96, 114, 115
Steps of Trool, Battle of, 102
Stevenston, 128
Stewart family, 79
Stewarton, 135, 150
Stinchar, River, 40, 55
Stirling, Battle of, 56, 100
Stoneykirk, 69

Straiton, 40, 48, 59, 162
Stranraer, 58, 65, 68, 69, 136, 140, 152, 171
Swan, Rev. David, 96
Sweetheart Abbey, 62, 86, 155

T
Tait, Saunders, 22
"Tam O' Shanter", 34, 47, 53, 158
Tam O' Shanter Inn, 139, 160
Tarbolton, 22, 37, 38, 42, 151, 166, 175
Tarfessock, 59
Tarff, River, 57, 63
Thomson, Peggy, 21
Thornhill, 52, 154, 167
Threave Castle, 153
Threave House, 153
Tongland Power Station, 61
Trool, Glen, 60, 90, 102
Trool, Loch, 56, 90
Troon, 43, 123, 133, 147-8, 151, 163
Turnberry, 101, 152, 153, 162
"Twa Herds, The", 95, 164
Twynholm, 130

U
Uchtred, Lord of Galloway, 78, 84
Urr, River, 57, 62, 63

V
Valley, River, 60

W
Wallace, Sir William, 56, Ch. VI, 122, 164
Wallace family, 77, 122
Waterside, 46
Welsh, John, 87
"Wet Sheet and a Flowing Sea", 168
Whitehaugh Water, 45

Whithorn, 67, 81, 82, 83, 84, 171
Whithorn, Isle of, 67, 82, 83, 149, 152, 155, 171
Whyte, Rev. Hugh, 91
Wigtown, 64, 67, 74, 86
Wigtown Bay, 64, 67
Wigtown Martyrs, 90
Wigtownshire, 39, 56, 64-9, 71, 74,
78, 97, 111, 112, 113, 116, 119, 137, 147, 153, 170-1
Willie's Mill, 22
Wilson, John, 22, 37
Wilson, Margaret, 90
Windy Hill, 90
Windy Standard, 59
Wright, Robert Patrick, 122